2001

TRADITION
REDISCOVERED

◆

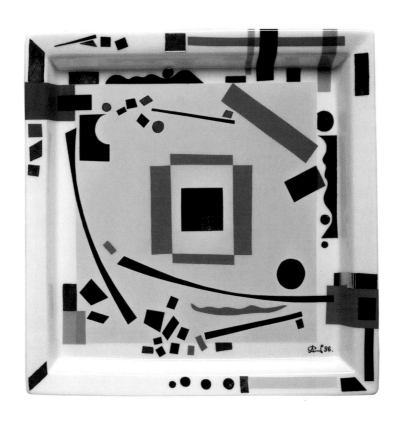

TRADITION REDISCOVERED
◆
THE FINLEY COLLECTION OF RUSSIAN ART

COMMONPLACE PUBLISHING

New Canaan, Connecticut

Dedicated to Harrison and Wilma Finley

This book has been produced
by CommonPlace Publishing
New Canaan, Connecticut

Editors: Lory Frankel, Cathy Suter
Art Director: Samuel N. Antupit
Designer: Tania Garcia
Printer: Oddi Printing Corp.
        Reykjavik, Iceland

Page 1: Untitled Porcelain Tray II,
1996. Leonid Alexeevich Sokolov

Pages 2 and 3: The Song (Detail),
1995. Lilia Anatoliovna Dolganova

Page 6: In a Birch Forest (Detail),
1966. Yuri Petrovich Sanin

Library of Congress
Catalogue number 98-072343
ISBN 0-9651 645-3-5

© The Finley Collection
Chattanooga, Tennessee

CONTENTS

◆

PREFACE: THE FINLEY COLLECTION

4

LESSONS FROM PAINTING'S PAST

6

THE RUSSIAN ACADEMY: A VITAL TRADITION

10

ARTISTS AND THEIR WORK

NOTES AND SOURCES

APPENDIX 1 AND 2

ACKNOWLEDGEMENTS

PREFACE: THE FINLEY COLLECTION

◆

In 1995, Lyle Finley was introduced to a wealth of painting that had long been locked behind the Iron Curtain. A successful businessman in Tennessee, Finley had developed a wide-ranging interest in art, including architecture, sculpture, and antique and contemporary furnishings and textiles as well as drawings, watercolors, and oils.

On the surface, there was nothing in Lyle Finley's background to predict his interest in Russian art. Born in Tennessee, Lyle grew up working in his parents' store, the J. H. Finley Supply, which provided Buffalo Springs and the surrounding area with food-stuffs, appliances, clothing, gasoline, and feed. It provided Lyle with a firsthand lesson in the fundamentals of successful retailing: supply and demand, customer service, and the importance of identifying and filling a niche in the community. All of these lessons, combined with his perseverance and capacity for hard work, came to the fore in a business venture he began with a friend, Ray Moss Jr., after graduating from college. After seeing a drive-through "milk jug" store during a vacation in Florida, Lyle and Ray decided to apply the concept to Tennessee. Both of them put in twelve- to fifteen-hour days day after day, week after week, until they had swelled their enterprise to fifty-nine stores.

In the mid-1970s, Lyle and Ray developed a full-service convenience store and expanded their product line by adding fuel. In 1976, Ray Moss Jr. died while flying his own airplane, and Lyle became the sole owner of the business. The stores now number 130, located in Tennessee and Georgia — including two of the original drive-throughs.

Lyle had excelled in sports in high school, winning a scholarship to college on the strength of his skills in baseball and basketball. These sports, not unlike his business, call for a commitment of time and energy as well as the abilities to work with a team and, at the same time, to take risks — to recognize an opportunity and go for it. These are qualities that Lyle brings to all his endeavors, even art collecting.

When art dealer Robert Garren showed Lyle the paintings he had brought back from the former Soviet Union, Lyle was attracted to the art and intrigued by the fact that most of the work had been unavailable up to that moment. In fact, it remained a major undertaking to bring it out of Russia.

Robert Garren, an art instructor at Southern Adventist University in Collegedale, Tennessee, with a master of fine arts degree from the Rochester Institute of Technology, had been making trips to Russia to buy art since 1995, a year after accepting a personal invitation to St. Petersburg to visit an artist he had sponsored at his college. As they made the rounds of St. Petersburg, they stopped at many artists' studios, where Garren saw work that impressed him with its quality and heard stories of the artists' plight in post-Soviet Russia.

Before the fall of Communism, the government had been the exclusive source of commissions for these artists trained at the state academies; suddenly, those commissions disappeared under the new government, which left the artists to fend for themselves in a "free" market that was more of a free-for-all yet placed daunting restrictions on the sale of their work, especially overseas. Anyone wishing to buy artworks and take them out of Russia had to spend several days dealing with paperwork and navigating the Russian bureaucratic maze before going through the hurdle of customs, where a tax of 100 percent of the work's appraised value (which might exceed the purchase price) was assessed. Even after complying with all the rules, a purchaser might be prevented from taking some artworks out of the country.

Garren decided to brave the obstacles and sell the art of his new friends in the United States. The first group of fifty paintings he brought back in May 1995 sold almost immediately. Since then he established the Garren Gallery and has made several trips to Russia each year to buy art.

Among his most enthusiastic clients was Lyle Finley, who responded to this art that, it seemed to him, reflected its makers' dedication to excellence and striving for beauty. His collection of Russian art grew until it represented the largest segment of his artworks, and it continues to grow. The best of it is offered here. ◆

LESSONS FROM PAINTING'S PAST

◆

With few exceptions, the artists represented in the Finley Collection were educated in St. Petersburg, at either the Repin Institute of Painting, Sculpture, and Architecture or the Academy of Industrial Arts (the Mukhina), or in Moscow, at the Surikov Institute. Each of these institutions falls under the auspices of the Academy of Arts, a state-funded national organization and the highest educational and scientific center for the fine arts in Russia. While the supervision of the training of young artists is its chief preoccupation, the Academy of Arts also provides a context for theoretical discussion among artists, opportunities for exhibition, and a liaison between its members and the state. The Soviet incarnation of the Academy was established in 1947, one of its tasks being to implement the Party line in all matters pertaining to the fine arts. Frankly stated, its goal was to "combat formalism, naturalism, and other features of contemporary bourgeois decadent art"[1] in favor of a single exclusive style, Socialist Realism. This style had been defined by Joseph Stalin's cultural henchman Andrei Zhadanov as not simply the transcription of objective reality but, rather, the revelation, by heroic, celebratory, even romantic means, of the revolutionary *potential* of reality. "Truth and historical concreteness of the artistic depiction," Zhadanov declared, "must be combined with the task of the ideological transformation and education of the working people in the spirit of Socialism."[2] Examples of this officially sanctioned style in the Finley Collection include the extensive suite of head studies and single figure paintings of the 1950s and 1960s by the late Mikhail Likhachev, an artist who trained in the studio of one of Stalin's favorite painters, Boris Ioganson.

As can be seen in much of the collection, however, the political changes of the last two decades — glasnost, perestroika, and, finally, the collapse of the Soviet Union altogether in 1991 — have shifted the focus of the Academy away from the singular hegemonic style it had nurtured toward a greater stylistic pluralism. At the same time, these political changes have allowed what was previously known as "underground" art — that is, any form of nonofficial or nonconformist art produced since the 1960s — to take center stage. The accompanying slide of the once all-powerful Academy, the bastion of "aboveground" art, has engendered a feeling in some quarters that the tables have now been turned: that the institution that formerly had the full approbation of the Party is now in the position of outcast. But this is mythmaking in the extreme: the dichotomy of underground and aboveground is not, historically speaking, a symmetrical one, and therefore it cannot be merely reversed. No matter how maligned by the newly mainstream (now former) underground, the Academy continues to occupy a position of great authority in the cultural landscape of Russia.[3]

The present-day Academy, in any case, has a much longer history than its Soviet incarnation might suggest. Its history may be traced back to the reforms of the early eighteenth century in which Peter the Great sought to refashion every aspect of Russian life according to European principles and taste. In the realm of art, this meant the importation of Neoclassicism, a mode of artistic expression in vogue throughout Europe in the eighteenth century that was based on the imitation of models drawn from classical antiquity (ancient Greece and Rome), the Renaissance (Michelangelo and Raphael), and the early Baroque (Poussin). When Catherine the Great founded the first Russian Academy of Arts in St. Petersburg in 1757, uppermost in her mind was the Académie Royale de Peinture et de Sculpture established in Paris a century earlier. Like the many academies organized in European centers in the seventeenth and eighteenth centuries, the Académie

All notes will be found on page 206.

Royale had its roots, in turn, in Italian precedents of the sixteenth century.

In tracing the history of the institution in which many of the Finley artists were trained, a whole slew of questions emerges for discussion. What is an academy, and how does it differ from earlier institutions for the training of artists? To what doctrines or principles does it adhere, and in what ways are these manifest in the paintings shown in this book? How might we best construe the complex relationship of academic practice in Russia to contemporaneous modernist and avant-garde experiments, on the one hand, and to postmodernism, on the other? Consideration of these questions will shed some light on the context in which much of the work represented here was produced.

Plato is said to have taught his students philosophy in the shade of an olive grove called *Akademeia*, a fertile place just outside the ancient city of Athens. During the Italian Renaissance, the name of this ancient grove, renowned for the disciplined training of the intellect that had taken place there, was adopted as the nomenclature for a new kind of institution for the education of visual artists. The first such "academy" was the Accademia del Disegno, established in Florence in 1563 with Michelangelo as one of its titular heads. What distinguished the Accademia from earlier institutions for the training of artists, such as guilds in which each student would be apprenticed to a particular "master," was its concern not only to foster manual skills but also to nurture and discipline the student's intellect. The latter involved a course of study with a range of instructors in such theoretical subjects as mathematics, perspective, geometry, anatomy, and natural philosophy, all of which would then be brought to bear on the student's acquisition of the practical skills of drawing and composition. The academy, therefore, was an important instrument in the humanist elevation of painting and sculpture from the realm of the artisanal trades to the pantheon of the liberal arts.[4]

The cornerstone of all academic training in the visual arts is the doctrine of imitation. As one of Michelangelo's pupils defined it, *imitation* means "to make a thing not only as another has seen the thing to be (when that thing is imperfect) but to make it as it would have to be in order to be of complete perfection."[5] Imitation thus involves the perfection rather than the transcription of appearances. This doctrine governs the three most important activities of the student's practical experience, which is organized into the form of a hierarchical progression, taking several years to complete, through tasks of increasing difficulty: first, drawing after the old masters (beginning with the copying of drawings and engravings and then proceeding to the copying of entire paintings); second, drawing after the antique (copying ancient Greek and Roman marbles or plaster casts of them); and finally, life drawing (after the nude model posed in the studio). With regard to copying after the antique, Svetlana Terentyeva's bronze (see page 174) provides an example of strict adherence to the ancient model, in this case to one of the most renowned of all Greek marbles, the *Venus de Milo*. Since its rediscovery in the early nineteenth century, the *Venus de Milo* has served as an exemplum for the creation of balance without stasis: by shifting the weight of the figure onto one leg while relaxing the other (which gives a twist to the body and throws off the symmetry of shoulder and hip), the ancient sculptor creates not only equilibrium in the pose but also the sensation of motion just arrested.

The first two exercises, which instruct through the imitation of canonical works of the past, provide the student with the requisite preparation to enable him or her to "perfect" the raw nature eventually encountered in the life-drawing studio according to an "ideal" form of nature sanctioned by classical tradition. Of the drawings in the Finley Collection, the young Nikolai Blokhin's capable rendering in sepia of a standing male nude (1995; see page 28) demonstrates that the "academy figure," as drawings generated in life studios are known, remains central to instruction at the Repin.

But what is especially remarkable about those artists trained under the auspices of the present Russian Academy is the breadth of their embrace of the academic doctrine of imitation. Instead of confining themselves to the imitation of the narrow canon of ideal beauty enshrined by academies in the past — a canon consisting, essentially, of the work of Raphael — the majority of the Finley artists have imitated a great range of historical styles, raiding the phenomenal collections of the Hermitage, and incorporating even those modern styles that are conventionally regarded as antithetical to the classical tradition. For example, Vasily Bratanuke's portraits of the late 1980s are explicitly Cézannesque in both the posing of the figures and the vigorous yet controlled working of the surface. The artist himself draws our attention to this debt in his *Portrait* (1989; see page 32), by posing his sitter in front of his own interpretive rendering of Paul Cézanne's *Still Life with Curtain and Flowered Pitcher* (c. 1899), a painting in the Hermitage, presumably copied by Bratanuke in situ. Lilia Dolganova, also from the Repin Institute, looks to other Post-Impressionist painters, such as Vincent van Gogh, and the Nabis symbolists, like Paul Sérusier, for her inspiration (*Still Life with Sunflowers,* 1996 and *The Song,* 1995; see page 34).

In the case of Victor Donskoi, a graduate from the Surikov, we witness the imitation of a range of different styles within the work of a single artist: his historical genre paintings (see pages 37 and 41) are reminiscent of several works in the Hermitage by Pieter Brueghel the Younger, while his *Play, Accordian* (see page 37) is suggestive of a whole panoply of Northern masters such as Brueghel, Frans Hals, and James Ensor. In the 1990s, even Socialist Realism is ripe for imitation: consider, for example, Donskoi's *Harvest* of 1994 (see pages 40–41), which portrays agricultural labor in that style's joyous, heroic, and celebratory modality. To a considerable extent, the same modality likewise suffuses Nikolai Repin's *With Victory* (1995; see page 122).

A similar range is evident in the work of Yaroslav Kurbanov, but here within a single painting. The very particular compositional structure of his *Artist and the Muse* (1992; see page 74), with its view into depth through three Romanesque arches immediately returns the viewer to Jan van Eyck's *Virgin and Child with Chancellor Rolin* (c. 1431) or to the work of any number of Flemish painters who adopted van Eyck's composition (such as Rogier van der Weyden, a version of whose *Saint Luke Drawing a Portrait of the Virgin* is in the Hermitage). In the same painting, Kurbanov's meticulous rendering of the silk folds of his muse's dress is unmistakably a tribute to the great seventeenth-century Dutch master of such finishes, Gerard Ter Borch (see, for example, the Hermitage's *Glass of Lemonade* or *Portrait of Catrina van Luenink*). On the other hand, for his *Female Nude* of 1996 (see page 76), Kurbanov composes a frankly mannered mise-en-scène that borrows from Giorgio de Chirico.

Daud Akhriev, however, is perhaps the most precociously versatile of all the painters represented here. In *Near Ponte Rialto* of 1996 (see pages 26–27), the cursive, moody dappling of water brings to mind Monet's Impressionism of the 1870s, while the lilac suffusion that signifies the shadow cast over the background summons the French painter's work of the 1890s, especially his London series. But it is with the several half-length or seated figure paintings of women in three-quarter view that Akhriev broaches the very dialectic of nature and artifice that underpins the doctrine of imitation itself. Consider *Girl with Turban* (1995; see page 26), in which the deliberately overly made up flesh of the face shares in the ornate hues of both the luxurious cloth in which the figure is wrapped and the theatrically staged Venetian backdrop before which she appears. In the self-conscious way in which the figure runs her ornament of pearls through her hands, Akhriev has captured something of the conspicuous artifice — the *maniera* — that bespeaks late-sixteenth-century Venetian or Ferrarese, rather than Florentine or Roman, precedent. The elongation of the neck of his *Ulricha* (1990–91; see page 24) brings to mind J.-A.-D. Ingres's eccentric anatomies, while the sumptuous Orientalizing costuming of *Mariat* (1997; see page 24) harks back to any number of nineteenth-century French Orientalists of academic persuasion, such as Jean-Léon Gérôme.

It is important to note, therefore, that although students enroll "u kogo-to" at the Russian Academy's institutes in their third year (that is, each enters into the studio of a specific professor, which might suggest a return to the preacademic apprenticeship model for the training of artists), this alliance does not extend to imitation of the professor's style per se. At least ten of the Finley artists, for example, were students in the studio of the famous academician Andrei Mylnikov, who has been teaching at the Repin for some fifty years, but their work is, stylistically speaking, very diverse and manifestly independent of his. In the hands of these Academy-trained artists, the doctrine of imitation is instead played out in the production of virtuoso demonstrations of what might best be described as stylistic eclecticism. Implicit in these demonstrations is faith in the notion that style can be detached from the historical context of its emergence, mastered through years of intense training, and then redeployed. In other words, style transcends history. This conviction is not exclusive to the Finley artists but is, in fact, fundamental to the way in which academic instruction has traditionally been organized around a "canon" of great works granted transhistorical or universal value.

As is well known, however, the principle of stylistic eclecticism has not gone unchallenged in the history of either the academy in general or the Russian Academy of Art in particular. Antagonism toward eclecticism was an important aspect of the more comprehensive revolt in the nineteenth century, fomented within the academies themselves, it should be noted, against the Neoclassical rules concerning appropriate subject matter and modes of execution. Set into motion early in the century by Romanticism, the revolt against academic strictures gained strength at midcentury with the Realists, who demanded both the inclusion of subjects drawn from contemporary life and a greater naturalism (that is, less idealism) in their depiction.

In Russia, these demands reached a crisis point with the famous "Rebellion of the Fourteen" in 1863, in which a group of artists led by Ivan Kramskoi resigned from the Academy in protest.[6] Hostility to the Academy steadily grew over the course of the next few decades, and in the 1890s, in order to stave off a full-scale crisis, the Academy invited onto its faculty a number of Realist artists that had once been students within its ranks, the most famous among them being Ilya Repin — the Repin Institute's namesake. A further aspect to the gradual relaxation of academic training around this time was the recognition, finally, of landscape painting as an academic subject. Before this, landscape had been excluded from the curriculum because, unlike history painting (which reigned over the hierarchy of subject matter), it did not involve the composition of figures into narrative or allegorical tableaux. Undoubtedly, therefore, the two late-nineteenth-century "reforms" are not unrelated; both the Realists' demand for a greater naturalism and the promotion of landscape painting contest the academic doctrine that the painter must portray nature not as it appears but as it "ought to be." Certainly, the body of landscape painting among the Finley artists, particularly the work of the late academician Piotr Fomin, Fyodor Zvonarev, Natalia Repina, Yuri Sanin, Anatoly Nebolsin, and Vladimir Shedrin, indicates a turning away from the concept of perfecting nature integral to the academic doctrine of imitation.

Like their French counterparts, the Russian Realists of the 1860s were artists who had survived the rigors of the academic system and then spurned its strictures in order to put their education directly in the service of the mounting struggle, in the social and political arena, against the stratification and degradation of the poor in contemporary Russian society. We should keep this fact in mind — that the Realist revolt came from within the Academy — when seeking to understand the relationship between academic and modernist artistic practices, a relationship conventionally thought of as exclusively antagonistic. In part this perception of antagonism has to do with the fact that the backlash against academies begun in the nineteenth century has been gathering strength ever since. In his groundbreaking study of the history of the European academies first published in 1940, Nikolaus Pevsner acknowledged the overwhelming predominance of an "anti-academic attitude" among progressive artists, but defended his subject on the grounds that it constitutes an important historical phenomenon in the social history of art, since from the Renaissance until the late nineteenth century almost all artists had been trained in academies.[7] In the 1960s, the kind of anti-academicism described by Pevsner reached its peak with the widespread rejection of life drawing and of academic art education in general.

As a consequence of the increasingly negative connotations of the term "academic," scholars have tended to place in opposition academic tradition and the various modernist movements that emerged in reaction to it — Impressionism, Post-Impressionism, Fauvism, Cubism, and so on — movements that emphasized the medium of painting itself over its capacity for illusion. The standard terms of this opposition may be succinctly summarized with reference to two paintings of the 1860s: in the French academician Adolphe-William Bouguereau's *Birth of Venus* of 1863, the artist's brush "licks" the entire surface of the illusion of its ostensibly mythological subject to a perfection of finish and transparency, whereas in Monet's *La Grenouillère* of 1869, a deliberate but rapid calligraphy composes each figure with two, or at most three, movements of the brush. Bouguereau's finish ensures that the viewer's attention will not be distracted from the subject, whereas Monet's economy deliberately interrupts the illusion of this scene of contemporary Parisian bourgeois leisure in order to highlight the materiality of the pictorial surface itself.[8]

Notwithstanding the strength of the opposition just noted, the dynamic between the Realists and their alma mater also characterizes, to a certain extent, that between modernism and the academy.

Many of the major proponents of modernism, such as Edgar Degas, van Gogh, Georges Seurat, and Henri Matisse, began their education in the academy and/or produced "academy figures."[9] Further, Matisse spent much of the 1890s in the Louvre making strict academic copies of paintings by Jean-Baptiste-Siméon Chardin, as well as more "interpretive" copies after Jan de Heem, as did van Gogh after Eugène Delacroix.[10] In the 1930s, Jackson Pollock paid his dues at the altar of tradition with a suite of charcoal and pencil drawings after Michelangelo, Signorelli, Brueghel, Rubens, Rembrandt, and El Greco.[11] The crucial point to be made, however, is that for these modernists, academic education was but a means to an end — a training undertaken in order to be surpassed. Except in extreme cases of avant-garde iconoclasm, such as Filippo Tommaso Marinetti's Futurism, the modernist invention of new stylistic devices is profoundly a matter of dialogue with, rather than outright rejection of, tradition. The violence perpetrated on the academic convention of the nude by Picasso and Matisse in the first decade of this century is, therefore, a double-edged sword: it simultaneously desecrates and revitalizes that tradition.

Furthermore, unlike the stylistic eclecticist who slips back and forth through history, the modernist conceives of history in terms of progression and, in the most extreme cases, of teleological progression. The modernist's ambition (in contrast to the academician's) is to take the *next* step, to surpass tradition in order to stake out one's own place within it. Grating hard against the academic doctrine of imitation is, therefore, the modernist's invocation of originality.[12] The academically trained Finley artists have learned to imitate tradition in order to preserve it more or less intact. For the modernist, on the other hand, the surpassing of tradition is the only means by which to keep tradition, in the end, alive. What has happened, however, is that modernist anti-academicism ultimately has come to constitute a new, alternative tradition, a "modern tradition." Hence, as we see in Bratanuke's work, the once transgressive force of Cézanne's style is muted, the controversy that surrounded its inception falls silent, so that the French painter's style may become yet another exemplar for imitation.

But modernism's putative "doctrine" of originality and its censure of stylistic eclecticism has, in turn, been challenged during the course of its history, most recently in the 1980s with the groundswell of self-conscious pastiche, appropriations, quotations, and reshufflings of the style-deck that is generally labeled *postmodernism*.[13] A Westerner unfamiliar with the context in which the Finley paintings were produced might tend to slot many of them, especially those of the Kurbanov brothers and Akhriev, within postmodernism's critique and rejection of modernist originality. This would be, however, to foist on these pictures an alien context, a discourse far removed from their very real ambition. This work is not postmodern, just as it is not modern, although it may quote modern styles — or, perhaps one should say, *precisely* because it quotes them. The Academy-trained do not go so far as to embrace the deeply cynical (even if also sometimes celebratory) argument that underpins postmodern appropriation art, whether of the retrograde or the progressive variety[14] — namely, that style is but an empty signifier. Nor do the academic artists extend their stylistic eclecticism to areas of visual practice lying beyond the sanctified realm of fine art, to incorporate, say, popular culture and the mass media, which are important sources for appropriation artists as diverse as David Salle, Juan Davila, Cindy Sherman, and Yasumasa Morimura. Instead, the traditional division between high and low is maintained: the sources of the Academy-trained all hail from the history of art as it has been conventionally defined, whether academic or modern.

Thus, a more than superficial analogy between the stylistic eclecticism of the Academy-trained Finley artists and the appropriation practices of the postmodern artists of the 1980s cannot be drawn. The free citation of past styles evident in much of the work in this book can only be understood within the context of its production — that is, the disciplined embrace of the doctrine of imitation, the cardinal principle of all academic instruction. This is an approach to the craft of painting that has enjoyed a long, varied, and often august history over more than four centuries. While the mainstreaming of the avant-garde in the postwar period has increased the public following for more self-consciously innovative forms of artistic practice, academic painting nevertheless continues to thrive, not only in surviving state institutions such as the Russian Academy of Arts but also in privately financed schools in many parts of the world. ◆ — *Maria Gough*

THE RUSSIAN ACADEMY:
THE CONTINUITY OF A VITAL TRADITION

◆

The Western art world has long been aware of the dissident, or underground, art of the Soviet Union. The fall of Communism has revealed a very different art — that of its "aboveground," academy-trained artists, dedicated to the goal of creating beautiful, sincere works employing superlative technique.

Assembled since the collapse of the Soviet Union, the Finley Collection reflects the education and lives of a specific group of painters trained in St. Petersburg, Voronezh, and Moscow, whose experiences may vary from those of artists trained in other Soviet cities or disciplines. Instead of the fervently patriotic pieces that the West might expect of Russian aboveground artists, this collection's strength resides in nonpolitical pieces created by the artists not as martyrs in a totalitarian regime, as pawns in an ideological struggle, or as artists isolated and behind the times, but simply for their own gratification. The Finley Collection offers portraits of the artists' families and friends, still lifes, and landscapes from all over the Eurasian continents. Artworks span both Communism and commonwealth (from 1944 through 1997), and the artists who executed them come from many of the nations that made up the Soviet Union as well as Russia. Common ground for all these artists, however, is that they share a Russian academic art training. It is this training that sets them apart from their Western contemporaries.

The most notable aspect of an art education in the former Soviet Union is its exhaustive duration. Individuals desiring to become artists there may attend middle art schools (grades six through twelve) devoted primarily to art education, four-year art colleges, and up to eight years of higher education at academies and institutes whose quality and curricula are supervised by the Russian Academy of Arts. This course of study from elementary level through postgraduate studies is available not only for students of

the fine arts but also for those wishing to pursue the decorative arts.

Many might question the benefits of up to fourteen years of academic training, and still others question the value of any academic training whatsoever. Andrei Mylnikov, artist and head of the mural painting studio at what may be Russia's most prestigious academy, the Repin Institute, St. Petersburg, for almost fifty years, has a ready explanation:

> It is difficult to imagine that some orchestra conducted by . . . Rostropovich might suddenly take into the violin section some person who had walked up to the concert hall out of nowhere. It doesn't work that way. They take the most wonderful violinists into the orchestra. . . . And why should an artist be any different? Why should an artist have less stringent training than a first violinist? . . . Anatole France said, "There are two monsters. A master who is not an artist, and an artist who is not a master." No one can teach a person to be an artist, but an artist should strive to become a master. Artists need a school to show them things, to understand the laws of nature, the most complicated of which are the laws governing the form of the human body.

All over the Soviet Union, artists from middle art schools to postgraduate programs are endeavoring to become masters. The Finley Collection presents evidence of their mastery.

THE ACADEMY OF ARTS AND ITS ACADEMIC CURRICULUM

One of the instruments for maintaining the system of art education in the Soviet Union/Russia has been the Academy of Arts, founded in 1947. It is a prestigious national organization comprised of 90 members and 150 correspondent members who advise the government on matters of culture. Perhaps its most important task is overseeing the art academies and institutes, most notably the Repin and Surikov institutes. The Academy of Arts designs and supervises one unified curriculum for all of its institutions, setting guidelines regarding everything from the sequence of drawing assignments to entrance examination criteria.

Students between the ages of sixteen and thirty-six may apply to Academy of Arts institutes annually. Applicants bring a portfolio of drawings, paintings, or sculpture and compositions (narrative artworks executed on a specific theme) to a selection committee, which meets once a year before the entrance exams. Based on the applicants' portfolios, the committee decides who will be allowed to sit for the week or more of entrance exams in competitive drawing and painting. Some students compete for several years before being accepted.

Those who make it (perhaps one in five who sit for exams) face six years of progressively more difficult work in drawing and painting or sculpting of the figure, under master teachers who give explicit instructions on how pieces should look and who expect obedience. School is in session from nine o'clock in the morning until five o'clock in the evening, six days a week, and the curriculum core for studio artists is a minimum of five hours a day spent working from life (models or still life). Students must also fulfill composition assignments, present artworks done outside the classroom, and acquire experience in other media, such as printmaking, mosaic, fresco, and sgraffito. At the same time, they take classes in anatomy, perspective, and art history.

Posing the model is a lengthy process undertaken with great seriousness by the studio's entire teaching staff. They position a model or models on a podium, carefully selecting background draperies and props, to create a unified stage called a *postanovka*. When the *postanovka* is completed, the models occupy their spot on the podium every day for more than a month for three hours of painting and two of drawing. Students draw and paint *postanovki* (the resulting compositions) in only natural, northern daylight (except on short winter days). *Postanovki* can be quite elegant and naturalistic, as in Genady Ulybin's *Female Model* (see page 186), or arbitrary and surrealistic, as evidenced by Yaroslav Kurbanov's *Female Nude* (see page 76).

Twice a year, a ceremony called *prosmotr* (viewing) transforms the academies into galleries. At the end of each semester the professors sort each student's body of work, picking out the best pieces to be hung on the wall. A committee of professors and administrators tours each studio, covered from floor to ceiling with artworks, and writes a grade on each piece. Students also take oral academic examinations at the end of each semester.

For the first two years, students spend most of their time on technical exercises. Although they draw the figure and produce portraits, zealous new students, eager to create grand paintings, often despair at the tedium of spending hours in the anatomical lecture room copying casts and bones, delineating skeletons, hands, and feet in ten different positions, and painting endless still lifes composed by the instructors.

Third-year students move to different quarters within the institute that offer them bigger studios, better light, and more models. While one teacher instructs each group of first- and second-year students, a large team converges on the more advanced students, and third-year students paint with the students ahead of them. The major professor, who supervises junior and senior instructors, appears with his entourage twice a week to monitor the progress of each student.

Academy of Art institutions have a short school year — October through the end of May, with several breaks — but then there is the *praktika*, the two-month obligatory summer program. In order to experience painting in different light, first- and second-year students are sent to either the far north of Russia or the Black Sea to paint landscapes. Third-year students must copy an old master work in a museum under the direction of the restoration department. Students finishing their fourth year have the freedom to choose a project — designing and building a mosaic, for example — and fifth-year students must demonstrate that they have laid the foundation for their diploma project, designed to prove a mastery of technique in composition, color, and understanding of form.

The diploma project, which gives students a master's degree equivalent on completion, is an ordeal unto itself. At the beginning of the year, when students submit studies for the semester's composition assignment, fifth-year students show diploma studies instead. The subject matter, as well as the studies, must be approved by the major professor. By the end of the first semester a final scheme has been set. Students spend the second semester, when they are not in regular painting or drawing class, graphing out the enlarged image, collecting materials, conducting research, and working on drawings or detail studies. Students entering their sixth year, called *diplomniki,* are issued a private studio, which they can hold for their last year. They also have a budget for models, stretcher bars, and frames.

There is some predictability to the diploma projects undertaken every year. If the *diplomniki* are working in the mural painting studio, the diploma paintings tend to be mostly monumental (*monumental* refers not so much to scale as to materials appropriate to public spaces, such as stained glass, tapestry, fresco, sgraffito). *Diplomniki* not of Russian heritage are encouraged (although rarely is much encouragement required) to choose subject matter illustrating their own culture and landscape. Native Russians lean toward incidents from their history, peasant life, or folk motifs, yielding colorful and festive images of weddings, the harvest, fairy tales, and town celebrations of holidays (for example, Lilia Anatoliovna Dolganova's diploma painting *The Song*). Subjects from World War II persist, although the once abundant revolutionary war themes have disappeared. Biblical subjects and scenes of life in the court of the czars have gained popularity since glasnost.

Every year at the end of May and the beginning of June, students defend their diploma projects in front of a jury composed of ten to twenty people: members of the Russian Academy of Arts from Moscow and St. Petersburg, rectors of both the Surikov and Repin institutes, and all the *diplomniki's* teachers. Fellow students and the general public make up the audience. The *diplomnik,* standing near his or her diploma project, gives a personal introduction and a short statement about the chosen subject matter and materials. Then the student artist steps away, and an art historian who has previously inspected the work speaks for five to ten minutes about the project's strengths and weaknesses. (By tradition these art historians — often museum curators — lean toward generosity in these assessments.) The members of the jury may speak about the diploma work, and their speeches can be quite amusing. The last person from the jury to speak is the *diplomnik's* major professor. In closing, the *diplomnik* again takes the floor to voice acknowledgments to teachers, friends, and family and present flowers to professors. Grades are not decided until later, in a closed-door meeting. Graduates never receive grades lower than 3 (on a scale of 1 to 5), because any *diplomnik* who appears in

danger of earning a grade of 2 is encouraged to withdraw and try again the following year. The diploma artworks themselves remain at the institute, the property of the Fund, the archive within the art institutes that collects the best works at the time of the end-of-semester viewing for the permanent collection. (Many students now try to smuggle their works out of the building after the viewing, before the Fund's employees can collect them. Foreigners who buy student pieces might find the Cyrillic letter F written on the work in charcoal, indicating that their purchases are such escapees.)

After graduation, a few artists (fewer than 5 percent) from each class are invited to remain to teach or carry out one of two kinds of postgraduate work: *tvorcheskaya* or *aspirantura. Tvorcheskaya,* a creative fellowship, awards graduates a free studio within an institute so that they may work toward creative maturity and begin to make a name for themselves. Some among the numerous Finley Collection artists who received creative fellowships are Nikolai Blokhin, Boris V. Lesov, Veronica Repkina, and Svetlana Arkadyevna Terentyeva. Recipients of *aspirantura,* such as Yura Kalyuta, also are granted a free studio and a chance to establish themselves creatively, but they are expected to develop their skills as a future teacher of an Academy of Arts institution.

Those not offered postgraduate positions must settle down and begin a career like artists anywhere in the world. Some originally from the provinces return home, but artists who live in major cities enjoy many more career opportunities. Extremely lucky artists begin a career of international exhibitions and sales. Theater has proven very fertile ground for artists in St. Petersburg and Voronezh, hundreds of whom have found employment painting scenery and designing sets and costumes. Zenovy Yaklovich Korogodsky, a noted children's theater director in St. Petersburg, asserted that at his theater he regularly hired painters who were having a hard time making a living or who were too unconventional for the aboveground art world. Many Finley Collection artists confirmed the safety-net role that the theater played for artists.

THE REPIN INSTITUTE OF PAINTING, SCULPTURE, AND ARCHITECTURE

Over half of the artists in the Finley Collection were educated at the Repin. (Named in 1944 for the Russian painter and teacher Ilya Repin, 1844–1930, an artist who concentrated on Russian themes, the Repin has known a variety of names; see appendix 1.) Still little-known in the West, the Repin is perhaps the only academy of art in the world with an unbroken two-centuries-old tradition of academic training. In 1718 Czar Peter I authorized the organization of schools for artists and artisans in his brand-new capital of St. Petersburg. The school for artists was set up in the home of a certain Count Shuvalov, who accepted gifted students without requiring noble birth. In 1757 Catherine the Great brushed Count Shuvalov aside as a dilettante and refounded the Academy of Arts in a magnificent new facility built for her on Vasilyevsky Island. (A legend widely circulated at the Repin has it that when Czarina Catherine went with her architects Alexander Kokorinov and Vallin de la Mothe to review the finished building, she complained that she had commissioned an academy of art, not a stables, after which de la Mothe hanged himself in a stairwell. Some believe that his ghost still haunts the premises. It makes for a good story, but the rumor is unfounded, as Catherine herself died before Vallin de la Mothe did. The other architect, Kokorinov, died during the course of the project, but of dropsy, not hanging.)

The institution in its new form was designed to copy, and perhaps eclipse, the Ecole des Beaux-Arts in France, to which end instructors were sought from all over Europe. Painting, sculpture, and architecture instructors were primarily French and Italian, and the printmaking teachers German. Russian artists apprenticed with the Europeans in St. Petersburg or were sent to study in the European capitals so they could bring their skill and experience back to St. Petersburg. A relationship with Europe was further cemented by sending prize-winning graduates from the Repin to paint in Rome for a year, all expenses paid. The Repin received many foreign guests, such as the Swedish painter Anders Zorn, who, with his friend Sergey Diaghilev, the Russian ballet impresario, visited St. Petersburg in 1897. James A. McNeill Whistler studied at the institution in the mid-1800s while his father built railroads.

In April 1918, the Communist government appropriated the academy. In the years leading up to, during, and following the revolution, the Communist government encouraged and utilized avant-garde artists in politics and at the Academy of Arts. Soon after the revolution, the government decided that these artists were politically dangerous and expelled them from the academy. Many fled the country. Victor Kemenov's book *The USSR Academy of Arts*, published in 1982, provides the then-politically correct Soviet explanation for the about-face:

> Their [the avant-garde artists'] position was fallacious in that they sought only their own personal freedom and interpreted such freedom in an individualistic manner — not only as emancipation from the officialdom of Tsarist Russia and whims of bourgeois patronage, but also as the liberation of their personality from "shackling" social ideals, however noble and human, which served to promote social progress. (p. 25)

The government had decided that traditional forms of art better served its needs.

Because the Soviet government sponsored the Repin on the understood condition that it produce artists capable of fulfilling totalitarian objectives, the Repin today is strapped with a reputation as the St. Petersburg "citadel of Party art," as Danila Korogodsky put it. One hears rumors that during the Stalin years a quota of graduate projects had to depict Stalin's favorite themes. If these rumors are true, any reality behind them had faded in the years following Stalin's death. Yura Kalyuta, who was a student in the early 1980s, claims that by then there were almost no political works at the academy, and propagandist diploma paintings were already amusing history. But, until the early 1990s, the absence of garish propaganda within the institution confused no one into thinking that work that was critical of the government or overtly religious would be tolerated.

Today, the Repin offers six-year degrees in easel painting, mural painting, theatrical painting (easel painting and set design), sculpture, graphic arts (illustration and printmaking), architecture, and art history.

The Repin is housed in an enormous classical building, which, together with its grounds and outbuildings, occupies several city blocks on the banks of the Neva River, within walking distance of the Winter Palace. This central location allows students easy access to the Hermitage and the State Russian Museum. Aside from its studios and classrooms, the Repin has two libraries containing books and facsimiles of old master drawings; a massive museum that exhibits rotating selections from the Repin's permanent collection of two hundred years of diploma artworks; a plaster cast museum for drawing; an anatomical library and lecture room; a wood shop for making frames and stretchers; a lab for making artists' materials; a professional mosaic studio; an artists' materials store; a workshop for replicating sculptures in plaster; a cafeteria; and a gymnasium.

THE VORONEZH INSTITUTE OF ART

It is not surprising that Voronezh, two hundred and fifty miles south of Moscow, boasts so many painters of exquisite landscapes (exemplified by Fyodor Pavlovich Zvonarev, Yuri Petrovich Sanin, and Vladimir I. Shedrin in the Finley Collection). Landscape painters have as inspiration the Voronezh River, grainfields, cattle ranches, forests, and a "big sky" that would not be unfamiliar to an artist from Minnesota or Kansas.

Founded as a settlement in 1585, Voronezh was the diplomatic center between Russia and the east where prisoners were exchanged and envoys met. When Peter the Great saw the settlement in 1694 he was struck by its strategic location, on the waterway leading to the Black Sea and the Sea of Azov, and he decided to build his navy in Voronezh, bringing in shipbuilders from Holland and England. During World War II, Voronezh, which stood along a front line, was almost completely destroyed. Over 85,000 unexploded mines were left on its territory.

Rebuilt and restored, Voronezh has long had a four-year art college, but those artists looking to continue their studies traveled to Moscow or St. Petersburg. The economic changes in Russia after the dissolution of the Soviet Union and the increase in crime have made such pilgrimages very difficult, and the need for an art institute or academy to serve Voronezh and the surrounding region became evident to many. Voronezh attacked this problem by initiating a new faculty of painting with the Voronezh State Institute of Art (Voronezhskii gosudarstvennyi institut iskusstv) in 1994. This fine arts department is already in the process of becoming certified by the Russian Academy of Arts to be one of its official art institutes (like the Repin and the Surikov institutes). Sometime in the future, its title will become the Voronezh State Academy of Art.

The painting department at the Voronezh Institute of Art is small — about six students per class, a total student body of fewer than thirty — and so new that it has yet to graduate its first *diplomniki*. Nonetheless, the students fulfill assignments and requirements identical to those at any Academy of Arts institute. Teachers for the young academy were gathered from among accomplished artists working in Voronezh; the first painting professor, Andrei Bogachev, is a Repin graduate.

One of the artists in the Finley Collection, Mikhail Shpakovsky, is a student at the Voronezh Institute of Art, and his father, Vladimir, is the dean of the painting department.

THE ST. PETERSBURG STATE ACADEMY OF INDUSTRIAL ARTS (MUKHINA)

Parallel to the educational track offered fine artists by the Ioganson Middle Art School under the Repin Institute and the Repin is St. Petersburg's Middle School no. 190 and the State Academy of Industrial Arts (AIA) for those interested in the decorative arts. The AIA is known informally as Mukhina, after Vera Ignatievna Mukhina (1889–1953), the renowned sculptor of the Soviet period. Middle School no. 190 opened just a few decades ago as a training ground for future decorative artists, but the AIA came into being near the end of the nineteenth century, thanks to Baron Stieglitz, whose name the institution first bore. It was one of the first schools conceived specifically for teaching the applied arts. One of the original strengths of the school was copying and improvising from the motifs of antiquity. Also the brainchild of Stieglitz is the AIA's museum of decorative and applied arts. The baron gave his favorite students bulging purses and sent them around the globe to amass treasures for the museum's creation.

After World War II, many new departments were added at the AIA, including those of ceramics, woodworking, textiles, and metals. The woodworking department is called the department of "small architecture" in order to reinforce the role of structure; the ceramics department by tradition has as its director an architect, not a ceramic artist, since its goal is to make art, not vessels, and it was thought that an architect would influence the ceramists to be less reverent of the materials and more concerned with the creation of designs using form and color.

Although at different times the AIA offered a five-year rather than a six-year program, its regime does not differ much from that of the Repin. It does, however, approach similar exercises from a different perspective — that of design. Students put in the same hours of anatomy lessons and figure drawing, the *postanovki*, but the skills they acquire will be applied to industry. Vladimir Mikhailovich Vasilkovsky, head

Entrance to the Repin Institute. 1998

Entrance to the studios of Andrei Mylnikov where postgraduate students work; inside the Repin Institute. 1998

Second-year students at work in the Repin Institute's painting class taught by Yura Kalyuta. 1998

of the Department of Ceramics at AIA, described the difference between the way AIA artists and Repin graduates tackle a creative problem: "The Repin graduates scrutinize the subject matter lengthily. They take a very literary approach. At AIA we tend to rush to the decorative solution much more quickly." Repin graduate and sculptor Svetlana Terentyeva admits a difference between AIA sculptors and Repin-trained sculptors, asserting, "AIA sculptors tend to prefer drama, boldness, being eyecatching. The Repin sculpture is quieter, more classical and more serious." AIA graduates also receive more instruction than is offered at the Repin in how to transfer their designs to industry.

Application to the AIA is as strenuous as to the Repin, and the competition has been consistent over the last few decades: six applicants for every available spot. AIA is the obvious choice for artists wanting to study decorative disciplines not offered at the Repin, but fine artists such as sculptors and painters must choose between the two institutions. One consideration for students making that choice is that the Repin program is six years of strictly academic training. The AIA, while still providing a solid base of traditional figure work, allows creative solutions that veer away from academic representation.

Of the artists in the Finley Collection, Alexander Kremer, Irina Safranova, and Leonid Sokolov were educated at the AIA.

THE SURIKOV INSTITUTE

Moscow's Surikov Institute began in 1832 as a private class offering instruction in drawing from nature. (The Surikov was named in 1948 for the artist Vasili Ivanovich Surikov, 1848–1916, who specialized in epic paintings based on Russian history; for its history, see appendix 2.) The class, open to the public, was financially supported by the Moscow Art Society, whose members included Prince Golytsin, governor-general of Moscow. The society wanted to form the basis of an eventual academy of art. In the meantime, the semiofficial classes continued for years, preparing serious students for further studies in St. Petersburg. The Moscow drawing classes were modeled on those of the Repin (then the Academy of Arts). The teachers in Moscow received plaster casts and other materials for instructional use from St. Petersburg. Many of the early Moscow teachers were graduates of the Repin.

In 1865, the enterprise in Moscow earned the right to award diplomas and the title of artist. In 1947 it was sanctioned by the Academy of Arts as a full institute, offering six years of education and a master's degree. Like the Repin and the AIA, it sponsors a middle art school, the Moscow Middle Art School, for the city's artistically gifted children.

Because the Moscow school was so closely related to the St. Petersburg tradition at its inception, the artistic style of its graduates was quite similar to that of the Repin's. As time passed, however, the two schools diverged stylistically. Some believe that Moscow takes a painterly approach while St. Petersburg favors a graphic style. Judging by the love of line displayed by St. Petersburg–trained artists, that theory may have some truth in it. The geographic location of the two schools may influence their styles as well. Moscow, as the capital of an enormous country and a centralized government, is fast-paced and bustling with industry and commerce. St. Petersburg, a much smaller city with a more reserved lifestyle, is rich in fine arts, architecture, and connections to European culture.

PROFESSIONAL LIFE DURING THE SOVIET YEARS 1950–90

During the Soviet period the dominant force in the lives of aboveground artists was the Artists' Union. In *Contemporary Russian Art*, Matthew Bown described its vital role:

> Most artists are catered for by the Artists' Unions. The USSR Artists' Union is an umbrella organization which incorporates the separate artistic Unions of each Soviet republic, as well as the Moscow and Leningrad Unions. Membership in a Union is of considerable importance to an artist. It entitles him to a studio, gives him access to materials which may otherwise be impossible to obtain, and above all means he can deem himself a full-time artist. This is an important consideration in a country where failure to have a recognized job can render one guilty of the crime of "parasitism." (p. 21)

All government commissions were awarded through the Artists' Union. Leonid Sokolov, a St. Petersburg porcelain painter, remembers that because of the government policy requiring that an art commission be included in most industrial budgets, ". . . there were masses of government commissions. There were enough for everyone." According to him, the pay, while not fabulous, was perfectly adequate by the standards of the time. The commissions available varied from generic paintings of Stalin, Lenin, and their minions featured as the beloved leaders of the Soviet Union to entirely attractive commissions for restaurant friezes, subway decorations, and playground sculpture. Nikita Fomin tells an amusing story regarding a sculptor who had carried out a commission to execute multiple figures for the playground of a kindergarten. He got into an argument with the clerk at the Artists' Union office over his compensation. The sculptor maintained that the figures of the gnomes he had created were life-size, while the union clerk was quite sure that gnomes were much bigger, and that the sculptor should be paid only for half-life-size figures. Attracting a growing audience, they loudly debated the height of gnomes. (In the end the clerk relented, and the sculptor was paid full price for life-size figures.)

When executing commissions, union members did not even have to deal with clients, who might be ignorant of artistic principles, because a union committee — the Artists' Council — was responsible for matching artist to client and then monitoring the progress of the artwork. The artist's assignment was actually to please this committee of democratically elected colleagues, who then defended the commission to the client. More often than not, the client was content with the judgment of this board of professionals. If the client was dissatisfied, the Artists' Council, not the client, returned to the artist for revision.

Belonging to the Artists' Union conferred other substantial financial benefits. The union took the production of exhibitions entirely upon itself, and the Artists' Union Fund regularly purchased works from union exhibitions, as did the Ministry of Culture and regional museums of art. The union furnished emergency financial assistance to members, a benefit that Leonid Sokolov received on the birth of each of his two children. Svetlana Terentyeva mentioned that sculptors who belonged to the Artists' Union had their works cast at foundries with no thought to the cost. All-expenses-paid travel was a generously distributed privilege, whether on creative excursions into the wilderness or to union-run artists' compounds, such as the Academic Dacha southeast of Moscow, where studios, a cafeteria, and even models were provided. Union members were sent abroad. While most Soviet citizens were trapped behind the Iron Curtain, the Artists' Union was surprisingly proficient at sending its members around the Eastern bloc and to France and Italy.

Of course, the Soviet-era Artists' Union had another agenda besides enhancing the lives of artists. The union's bureaucracy provided a mechanism through which the art scene could be ideologically monitored — keeping the aboveground art world politically "safe" and ensuring that the underground art would remain just that. Some portion of the enormous pool of active artists that it sustained could be counted on for propaganda projects. Despite being the middleman between the government and the artists, however, the union appears to have served the government's ideological requirements only as far as necessary to keep the wheels greased while remaining firmly on the side of the aboveground artists.

During the Soviet period, artists had opportunities for lucrative and prestigious advancement. For those within the educational system, the career path, resembling that at an American institution, progressed from an *aspirantura* fellowship to junior teacher, full teacher, professor, head of studio, director of department, and rector. The government gave awards for artistic achievement, such as Honored Artist of the USSR, People's Artist of the USSR, the Lenin/Stalin Prize, and the State Laureate Prize, which raised the artist to a higher level of payment for commissions. One of the highest awards, election to the Academy of Art, brought not only prestige but also a salary in addition to whatever monies the artist already earned from commissions or teaching. Two academicians, Andrei Mylnikov and Piotr Fomin, and one corresponding academician, Vyacheslav Frantsevich Zagonek, are represented in the Finley Collection.

Soviet aboveground artists believed that their job was to create beautiful, sincere works, using superlative technique. They felt that artists should use the tangible power of art to enhance life. The artists' efforts to carry out their mission (and do what they loved) was supported wholeheartedly by the regime, which saw "beautiful" art as, first, a credit to the state and, second, politically benign and soothing to the population. Judging from the comments of Finley Collection artists, very few aboveground artists yearned to produce that which was forbidden. They considered a lifetime of perfecting still life, figurative pieces, and landscapes to be such an honorable and consuming task that it eclipsed all other considerations. Thus, the government and the aboveground artists were in agreement that artists have power morally to uplift the population, and that the artist should achieve this goal through beauty and relatively traditional technique.

Artists who became dissidents, of course, got into trouble with the Party. Those who turned their backs on their training and abandoned traditional technique and the goal of producing "beautiful" art were excluded from exhibits and financial opportunity. It was not unheard of for a Party member to storm through an exhibition demanding that a painting be ripped off the wall and the artist punished, but more often artists and the Artists' Union became self-censoring, reserving for private viewing works that might be overtly religious or critical of the government.

Some artists found the worst effect of the Communist regime to be the manipulation of rewards. All members of the Artists' Union, painting exactly what they pleased, were guaranteed the lowest standard of living. Upward mobility was often, if not invariably, triggered by presenting at least one grand patriotic work of art to the nation. After that, or perhaps after receiving an award or two, the artist's pay scale went up a level, commissions were guaranteed, and the artist was free of the Party and under no further obligation. Nikolai Trunov, who paints many landscapes and floral still lifes, commented, "I would be left alone in peace to paint as many bouquets and flower gardens as I wished, but I wouldn't ever see any Lenin Prize or award of Honored Artist of the USSR."

Marianna Borisovna Fomina, architect and widow of landscape painter Piotr Fomin, indicated that political pressures were never brought to bear on her husband regarding his output, and that as far as she knew, he had been responsible for his creative decisions every day of his life. Later, however, she recalled one incident. Fomin had submitted to an exhibition jury a landscape called *Partisans Slipping into the Forest,* depicting his native village during World War II. It showed a snowy clearing at the edge of a wood and bundled, armed volunteers departing for battle. Apart from them stood an old woman, holding up her arm and making the sign of the cross for their souls. Some friends of Fomin on the jury called him a few days later, very concerned. They asked him what in the world he thought this woman in the painting was doing. "What!" he said to them in mock astonishment, "You can't see that she's waving good-bye?" With that, everyone was mollified.

Students, restive after ten years or so of figure drawing, were more likely than mature artists to express curiosity about forbidden Western art. Daud Akhriev remembers as a student the sweet terror of passing around a blacklisted book of Salvador Dalí. According to Irina Safranova, artists in fashion design were starved for news of the latest international trends. Fashion design students and professionals knew exactly what few French magazines, unavailable to the general public, would be at which library on what day, and they devoured every word. But most Soviet aboveground artists did not feel the injury of isolation too deeply, since their relationship to modern art was not dissimilar to that of a curious spectator observing a circus freak. Vladimir Proshkin admitted, "I knew very little about Western art, but it is my own fault. If I had wanted to I could have gone to the library and studied up on it in magazines and periodicals, but I had no desire to do that. What happened in the West after Impressionism did not attract me." Many academy-trained artists felt the same way about their own artistic avant-garde from the time of the revolution — Kazimir Malevich, Natalya Goncharova, Vladimir Tatlin, El Lissitzky, Lyubov Popova, artists greatly admired in the West.

CONTEMPORARY PROFESSIONAL LIFE

The most common misconception that Westerners may have about Russian academy–trained artists is that life under Communism was an isolated hell for them, from which they have now been released into a free-market, democratic heaven. In fact, many artists claim that professional life for them was better between 1950 and 1991 than it is now.

The most obvious reason for this analysis is that the support offered to artists by the Artists' Union in St. Petersburg and Voronezh has disappeared in the last seven years. Its powerful role as the distributor of government commissions disintegrated, since there simply are no more government commissions. The former practice of both the union and the Ministry of Culture of purchasing works from Artists' Union members became obsolete as early as 1990, because high inflation significantly reduced their purchasing budgets. The sudden disappearance of income through the Artists' Union has been particularly punitive to women artists, for whom it is difficult to become entrepreneurs in addition to their responsibilities as mothers, housekeepers, caregivers, and artists. Travel to union creative compounds is still allowed, but artists must pay for their travel as well as room and board. Few artists can afford that. The rent charged members who hold studios continues to rise ominously. Previously stringent standards for membership have been lowered to embrace almost any candidate willing to pay annual dues of 60,000 to 80,000 rubles ($12 to $16). Admitting new members has the short-term effect of paying administrative costs, but the long-term result is that the group of members fruitlessly awaiting a studio from the union has doubled. Yaroslav Kurbanov said he would join the Artists' Union "just in case I might get a studio from them." He thought his odds of receiving a studio to be slightly higher than zero. In fact, when asked why one should be a member of the Artists' Union today, St. Petersburg artists replied that the four remaining benefits were to exhibit annually among one's peers, to maintain or hope for a studio, to enter museums free of charge, and to have a registered profession.

Democracy and the free market have come to these artists with very few of the benefits known in the West, and at a very high cost. So far no replacement has appeared for the vanished government commissions, museum purchases, and Artists' Union stipends. There is not yet much of a middle class, and the members of the famous Russian intelligentsia, although great art lovers, are themselves rarely solvent. Rumors have it that there is a healthy internal art market in Moscow, but the newly wealthy class in St. Petersburg and Voronezh rarely feels the need to buy original art other than "power portraits." New businesses have not displayed much desire to adorn their headquarters. Thus, it seems that foreigners are the primary art buyers, but neither the government nor the Artists' Union is of much help in facilitating sales to them. A prospective customer must wait until the conclusion of an Artists' Union show to purchase a piece. The act of purchasing a work of art through the Artists' Union can require quite an astonishing amount of paperwork, maybe more than one day's worth. Since checks and credit cards are not acceptable, only after cash payment may the foreign customer depart with a purchase. Aside from its inconvenience, this system simply does not allow a traveler who is in St. Petersburg for only a few days realistically to consider purchasing work from an exhibit. Russian customs is equally unhelpful, having placed an export tax of 100 percent on artworks, which frightens away more potential clients.

That the entire country is in complete financial chaos and that there is only the hint of a functioning banking system also affects the lives of the artists. One artist who recently married took out a three-year, low-interest loan for thirty thousand dollars from an entrepreneur for a new apartment with a studio, since it was impossible to get a bank loan for housing. A month after moving into their new accommodations, the couple found thugs at the door who announced that their employer had bought the loan from the original lender. If the loan was not paid within sixty days, the messengers threatened, bad things would begin to happen. Another artist saved enough capital to build a new studio in the country, but by the time the building was barely above ground, inflation had driven up prices so much that to continue was impossible. The artist lost his down payment. A third artist from this collection had an entire shipment of paintings held hostage in Russian customs for six weeks because the customs agents would not accept the bank checks sent from Germany to pay duty and the Germans would not fly over to pay in cash.

Institutions are no more immune to the enormous changes than individuals. The Repin's budget is so reduced that it cannot pay salaries regularly. Teachers, paid their "monthly" salary once or twice a semester, struggle to concentrate on the business of teaching while having to subsidize their incomes at second, and even third, jobs. With inflation, models' pay became so low that they deemed coming to work optional. In order to sustain the models, many studios have resorted to taking up collections from the students to augment the official pay. Likewise, at the AIA, most of the nonteaching staff stopped working when the school became unable to pay salaries.

Because of the difficulties of post-Soviet life, artists hesitated when asked if things had changed for the better for them. It is clear that they feel that their lives were certainly *simpler* before the changes. Many artists expressed frustration that being a competent artist is no longer enough for survival; they must also have business skills and connections in order to market themselves and plan for the future. The Communist Party's meddling in the creative process was inconsequential compared with that of hard-to-please private customers today. And still others despaired that the quality of art might decline as the artists attempt to appeal to masses with only a rudimentary understanding of aesthetics. Vladimir Proshkin complained, "Today the government does not want to help us but wants to take advantage of us. Everyone wants to take advantage of us. Even our own immigrants to other countries try to come and buy our work cheaply to take advantage of us. If the government, the one we had, made for us a tiny vacuum, where they said paint this, or even paint exactly what you want, then they made sure that you had good working conditions. The market [economy] just threw us out."

Even so, none of the artists chose to say that they would return to life under Communism. Many feel that their independence, no matter how unreliable, is sweet. Nikolai Repin (no relation to the namesake of the institute), a Repin Institute graduate and St. Petersburg artist, summed it up after a long period of careful thought: "I think democracy and a free market are probably a good thing. We just haven't figured out how to use them yet."

Some benefits of democracy and a free market are already evident to aboveground artists. They feel they have fallen into their rightful place as world citizens — coming and going and earning their way as do people in other nations. Artists who felt encumbered by the bureaucracy of the Artists' Union have had that burden lifted. Any artist may leave the country to exhibit or paint without securing permission. They may advertise their work. Those artists with the opportunity may start businesses and sell their work directly to foreigners — the origins of the Finley Collection. While under Communism artists benefited from a safety net, the system also controlled the upper limit of their earnings. With that limit removed, those who can may become rich and enjoy the same good things in life as wealthy individuals around the world. There is some evidence that a healthy banking system is just over the horizon, since one Finley Collection artist received payment for a purchase by international wire for the first time.

Most difficult to calculate is the value of the freedom now more or less available to everyone — freedom of thought, of speech, of choice, including, of course, of subject matter. In the post-Soviet era, some academy-trained artists are exploring newly permissible subject matter. Andrei Mylnikov and Nikita Fomin have completed several biblical compositions. Vladimir Vasilkovsky has a series of drawings and watercolors through which drift pop-culture images of Lenin. Leonid Sokolov is reinventing Constructivist motifs in his latest porcelain paintings. Artworks depicting the life of the Russian aristocracy and illustrating previously banned literature can be found in student work.

More changes may be in store. Now that there is no artificial division between aboveground and underground art, the two circles find themselves on the same playing field. Once almost hermetically sealed off from one another, and not a little suspicious of each other, the two camps now exhibit and compete for business side by side. The new fraternization has confirmed an old mutual condescension of some artists for their new comrades, but it has inspired grudging admiration among others.

Even considering their current experimentation, the political changes in Russia have provided formidable proof of the former aboveground artists' commitment to their academic training. It is true that the Communists pumped money into art schools, commissions, museums, and the Artists' Union. But the will to make "beautiful" art using traditional techniques has not vanished along with the Communist regime. Despite the new availability of nontraditional art career paths and the absence of government incentives, applicants continue to stream in to the academies and institutes of art. Young artists Vasily Bratanuke and Genady Ulybin say that they chose the Repin Institute specifically because of its academic tradition. Yura Kalyuta claims amazement at the dedication and performance of his students, especially the women, even though daily life is much more difficult for them than it was for him when he was a student.

The majority of academically trained professionals have not abandoned their ways in the new atmosphere of permissiveness. The traditional disciplines of figure work, landscape, and still life remain the focus of their attention. The artworks in the Finley Collection provide bountiful documentation of their commitment to technical accomplishment and the interpretation of nature, a tradition that dates back almost two and a half centuries in Russia and that shows every sign of continuing to be a dynamic force far into the future. ◆ — *Melissa Hefferlin*

DAUD M. AKHRIEV

(1959-   )

Daud M. Akhriev was born in 1959 in Kazakhstan where his family was in Stalin-imposed exile. Akhriev's nationality is Chechen-Ingush. From the age of eight, he studied at art grammar school and high school in Vladikavkaz. After his mandatory service in the army ended in 1982, Akhriev moved to St. Petersburg to audit classes in the studio of Andrei Mylnikov and take entrance exams to the Repin Institute. He was accepted in 1984 and later graduated under landscape painter Piotr Fomin. Following the defense of his diploma painting, Akhriev left for the United States. Since 1993 Akhriev has lived in Tennessee, painting and exhibiting throughout the United States and Europe.

Being Muslim from a small nation on the border between East and West has given Akhriev a love of painting intricate fabrics and rugs, men at prayer, and historical figures from his nation's past. For example, Akhriev's painting *Zelemkhan* (shown on the opposite page) is a portrayal of the legendary Chechen hero who performed amazing acts of bravery, physical prowess, and kindness. Zelemkhan fought the Russians

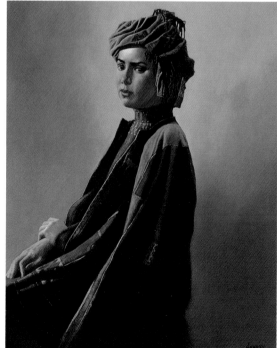

Ulricha, 1990–1991. Oil on canvas. 23 ½ x 31 ⅛ inches.

LEFT:
Mariat, 1997. Oil on panel. 14 x 11 inches.

OPPOSITE:
Zelemkhan, 1992–1993. Oil on canvas. 76 x 51 inches.

during the Chechen-Ingush war for independence at the turn of the century.

While living in Russia, the Caucasus, Tennessee, Minnesota, Germany, Italy, and Switzerland, Akhriev has painted an impressive variety of landscapes. His paintings are in the collections of numerous museums and institutions in the United States and Russia. Akhriev is married to American artist Melissa Hefferlin.

LEFT:
Girl with Turban, *1995. Oil on canvas. 18 x 24 inches.*

RIGHT:
Near Ponte Rialto, *1996. Oil on canvas. 11 x 14 inches.*

NIKOLAI BLOKHIN

(1968 –   )

Nikolai Blokhin was born in St. Petersburg in 1968 and knew from the age of thirteen that he wanted to be an artist. He studied at St. Petersburg's Middle Art School from 1981 until 1986, entering the Repin Institute in 1987. He graduated from the studio of Reikhet in 1995, after which he was immediately offered a postgraduate creative studio and a position at the Institute as a drawing teacher. Blokhin has been a member of the Russian Artists' Union since 1996.

Most famous for his drawings, Blokhin continues to attend Repin figure classes to keep his technique fresh. The period in art history to which he looks for inspiration is the Renaissance and he is particularly interested in the work of Velázquez.

Blokhin exhibits frequently throughout Russia and abroad. In 1995 his work was featured in a Moscow exhibit of postgraduate artists from the Repin and from Moscow's Surikov Institute. In the winter of 1995 and summer of 1996, Blokhin taught and exhibited in master classes. *Expressions from Russia*, an exhibit outside of Chattanooga, Tennessee, featured over fifty of his drawings.

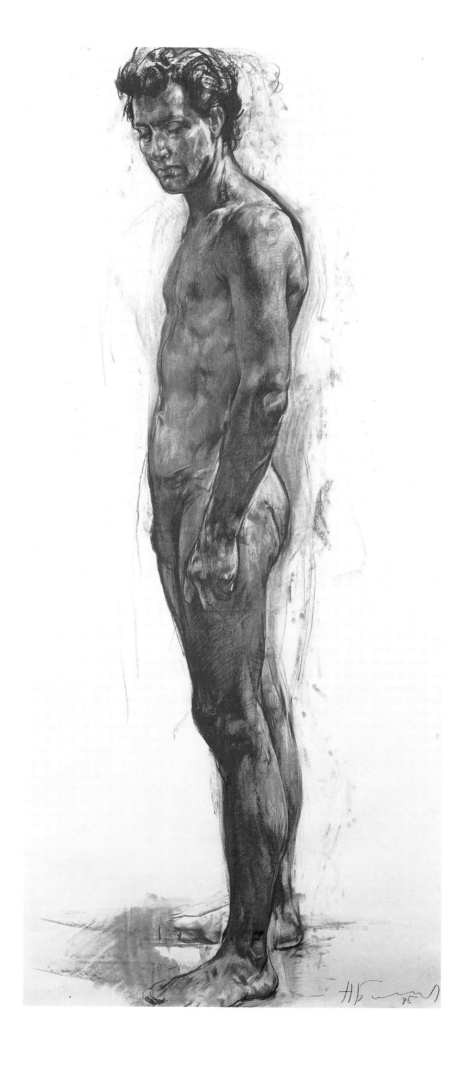

Female Portrait, *1996.*
Charcoal on paper.
57⅛ x 29 inches.

OPPOSITE:
Standing Model, *1995.*
Sepia on paper.
58 ½ x 29 inches.

ANDREI BOGACHEV

(1951–)

Andrei Bogachev was born in Saratov in 1951. He studied painting at the Repin Institute under Boris Ugarov and graduated in 1985.

Bogachev frequently works with still life, but is more actively involved with landscapes. Often he combines portraits with nature studies and his approach is looser than traditional Soviet realism. His colors are rich and there is a geometric turn to his brushstrokes.

Today Bogachev lives and works in Voronezh with his artist wife, Valentina. He is the painting professor at the Voronezh State Institute of Art.

The Dock, *1994.*
Oil on canvas.
27⅞ x 31½ inches.

Catfish, *1994.*
Oil on canvas.
27⅞ x 29¼ inches.

OPPOSITE:
Detail of Catfish.

VASILY IVANOVICH BRATANUKE

(1964–)

Vasily Ivanovich Bratanuke was born in the Ukraine in 1964. He began his art studies at the art school for children in the town of Starokosmanminov, Ukraine, and graduated from the Ukrainian Odessa Art School in 1984 with a degree in painting. He recently graduated from the studio of the late Neprintsov at the Repin Institute in St. Petersburg, where he now lives.

Although accomplished in many genres, he is best known for his striking portraits and paintings of ballet — his first love. "Ballet," he says, "is a source of moral beauty and spiritual thinking."

Paintings by Bratanuke have been exhibited and purchased in Bulgaria, France, Germany, Italy, the Netherlands, and the United States. His works are in museums in Lvov, Kiev, and Odessa.

An Uncle, *1984.*
Oil on canvas.
20½ x 19⁷⁄₁₆ inches.

Portrait, *1989.*
Oil on canvas.
22⅛ x 22 inches.

OPPOSITE:
Detail of Portrait.

LILIA ANATOLIOVNA DOLGANOVA

(1964–   )

Lilia Anatoliovna Dolganova was born in 1964 in the central Russian industrial city of Izhevsk, where she attended an elementary art school. From 1979 to 1983 she studied art at the Cheboksar Art College and continued at the Repin Institute, graduating in 1992. At the Repin she studied mural painting under Andrei Mylnikov, but was arguably more influenced by Mylnikov's colleague Alexei Sokolov, a painter of festive still lifes and expressive portraits, brilliant and whimsical in color.

Following graduation Dolganova was sent by the Repin to the Academic Dacha outside of Moscow to paint for two months. A member of the Russian Artists' Union, Dolganova exhibits with them around Russia. Dolganova's diploma painting, *The Song* (shown on the right), was included in a show of the best of the last three years' diploma paintings from the Repin and Surikov Institutes at the UNESCO exhibition hall in Paris in 1994. Works by Dolganova are in private collections in Europe, Russia, and the United States. Dolganova lives and works in St. Petersburg.

Still Life with
Sunflowers, *1996.*
Oil on canvas.
31¹⁵⁄₁₆ x 25⁷⁄₁₆ inches.

The Song, *1995.*
Oil on canvas.
47 x 39 inches.

OPPOSITE:
Detail of The Song.

Portrait of the Artist
Trunov, 1996.
Oil on canvas.
33¹³⁄₁₆ x 31⁹⁄₁₆ inches.

Play, Accordion,
1996. Oil on canvas.
58¾ x 72⁹⁄₁₆ inches.

Peter I at the
Voronezh Shipyard,
1996. Oil on canvas.
50¹⁵⁄₁₆ x 62¹³⁄₁₆ inches.

OVERLEAF:
Detail of Play,
Accordion.

VICTOR ANDREEVICH DONSKOI

(1945–   )

Victor Andreevich Donskoi was
born in Voronezh, Russia in 1945.
In 1960, he began to take classes in
a drawing studio where his teacher,
Evgeniya Romanovskaya, was the
first to predict he would become an
artist. In 1968, after four years in
the navy, Donskoi entered Penza
Art College from which he graduated with excellence in 1972 with a
recommendation to Moscow's
Surikov Institute. There he studied
in the studio of academician E.
Kibrik, and following his 1979
graduation he taught in several art
colleges in the Voronezh area.

Since 1980, Donskoi has had
access to several academic dachas,
including the one provided by the
Repin. He credits this experience
in nature for his development as a
painter and graphic artist.

Donskoi has been a member of
the Russian Artists' Union since
1985. He has recently been working
on paintings honoring the 300-year
anniversary of the Russian fleet as
well as a series of paintings
devoted to the joys of rural life.
He has exhibited every year since
1975 in Moscow and abroad. His

37

works are in collections in the United States, Canada, France, Spain, Italy, England, Germany, Scotland, South Korea, and Japan. Recently Donskoi visited the United States. He lives and works in Voronezh.

Menshikov's House in Front of the House of Peter the Great on the Land of Voronezh, *No Date.* *Oil on canvas.* *52 ¹³⁄₁₆ x 60 ¹¹⁄₁₆ inches.*

OPPOSITE:
The Harvest, *1994.* *Oil on canvas.* *50 ¹⁵⁄₁₆ x 62 ¹³⁄₁₆ inches.*

EDOUARD EFANOV

(1938 –)

Edouard Efanov was born near Voronezh in 1938, in the village of Khrenovoye under Bobrov. Efanov has lived all of his life in the Voronezh region, mostly in Ramon, a town 20 miles from Voronezh. In 1953, Efanov entered an art college in Elets. His teacher there was V. Sorokin, a known master of poetical landscape. Efanov later graduated from an art college in Saratov. After returning from military service in 1961, Efanov settled in Ramon. His first exhibition there was a success and opened doors for him. One of his paintings, *Drifting Ice,* was exhibited in regional and national shows.

As a child Efanov was greatly impressed by the beauty of constantly changing nature. This early experience is probably one reason why he is primarily a landscape painter today. The charm of his works lies in their light airiness, in the subtleness of his color combinations, and in the blending of Russian emotion with landscape painting.

The Two, *No Date.*
Oil on canvas.
19½ x 21⅛ inches.

OPPOSITE:
Boy with a Snowball,
1974. Oil on canvas.
59⅛ x 23¼ inches.

Snow is Leaving,
1979. Oil on canvas.
31½ x 55⅛ inches.

45

ALEXANDER EFIMOV

(1923–)

[no biographical information available]

Two Girls at School,
1966. Oil on canvas.
17⅛ x 22⅞ inches.

OPPOSITE:
Detail of Two Girls at
School.

VLADIMIR DMITRIEVICH FEFELOV

(1939 –   )

Vladimir Dmitrievich Fefelov was born in Vorashilovgrad (Lugansk) in 1939. He completed five years of college studies in painting and pedagogy in 1961 and is a member of the Artists' Union.

Fefelov is best known for his still lifes and for his expressionist portraits. His work is represented in the English art catalogue *Russian Gallery* and has been collected in England, France, Germany, Italy, Sweden, and the United States.

He participates in regional and national exhibitions.

Mushrooms, *1995.*
Oil on canvas.
27½ x 20¼ inches.

Still Life with
Kettle, *1990.*
Oil on canvas.
27¼ x 23¹¹⁄₁₆ inches.

49

Harvest Still Life,
1994. Oil on canvas.
27⅞ x 23⅛ inches.

50

Country Still Life,
1995. Oil on canvas.
29⅛ x 24 inches.

NIKITA PETROVICH FOMIN

(1948 –)

Nikita Petrovich Fomin was born in St. Petersburg in 1948. He is the son of the nationally revered landscape painter and academician Piotr Fomin, who is also a Finley Collection artist. After completing the Middle Art School Fomin studied at the Repin Institute, graduating from Andrei Mylnikov's mural painting studio. He became a member of the Russian Artists' Union, serving for years on a variety of union councils. He has received the State Laureate Prize of Russia for his paintings and is now the painting teacher in Eduard Kachirgin's theatrical painting studio at the Repin.

Fomin is a member of a four-person creative alliance called *FoRUS* (an acronym for its artists, Fomin, Repin, Uralov and Sukhov). Adept in fresco and mosaics as well as oil, these four artists collaborate to produce monumental artworks on commission.

Fomin has exhibited extensively throughout Russia as well as in Europe and the United States. He is married to Finley Collection artist Irina Safranova.

Bastille Square, *1991.*
Oil on canvas.
19¼ x 23½ inches.

PIOTR TIMOFEEVICH FOMIN

(1919–1996)

Piotr Timofeevich Fomin was born in the village of Lediakha in the Pskov region of Russia in 1919, but from 1931 he lived in St. Petersburg. After finishing art grammar and secondary schools, Fomin taught drawing in Leningrad, except from 1941 to 1945 when he fought in World War II against Germany. His graduation with honors from the painting department at the Repin Institute was in 1952, after which he taught for 43 years as head of his personal studio of painting at the Repin.

Fomin was adept at all genres of painting, but favored landscape throughout his life. A large portion of Fomin's landscapes were painted around his dacha, about eight hours' drive south of St. Petersburg, but he also traveled throughout Russia painting small villages, historic spots, and cityscapes. In addition he painted many landscapes on his travels through France, Italy, Finland, and England. Rarer than landscapes but no less exquisite are Fomin still lifes, usually informal, asymmetrical compositions featuring flowers from friends, fruit, and the porce-

Fall, 1995.
Oil on canvas.
35 ⅛ x 25 ⅜ inches.

Green Spring, *1991.*
Oil on canvas.
31⅛ x 29⅝ inches.

TOP RIGHT:
At Lake Lana, *1992.*
Oil on canvas.
34⅞ x 25⅜ inches.

BOTTOM RIGHT:
Untitled, *No Date.*
Oil on canvas.
23¹¹⁄₁₆ x 31⁹⁄₁₆ inches.

Still Life with Blue
Teacup, *1993.*
Oil on canvas.
19⅛ x 23¹³⁄₁₆ inches.

TOP LEFT:
Northern Fishing
Village in the White
Nights, *1993.*
Oil on canvas.
23½ x 32 inches.

BOTTOM LEFT:
Northern Village,
1995. Oil on canvas.
25⅝ x 35 inches.

lain cups from which he drank tea. Museums throughout Russia contain Fomin's narrative paintings of World War II.

From 1983 to 1991 Fomin was the rector of the Repin Institute. In 1977, he received the prized title of People's Artist of Russia, and in 1983, the State Prize of Russia for Artistic Achievement. His membership in the Russian Artists' Union began in 1952, wherein he served for some time as Chairman of the St. Petersburg chapter. His full membership in the Academy of Arts of the USSR was awarded in 1973. From 1952 on, Fomin regularly participated in exhibitions in the USSR and then in Russia, especially in Moscow and St. Petersburg. Large one-man exhibitions of Fomin's work took place in the State Russian Museum in St. Petersburg in 1984 and in the Central Exhibition Hall in Moscow in 1986, as well as in other cities.

Fomin paintings are in collections around the world: Moscow's Tretyakov Gallery, the State Russian Museum in St. Petersburg, the Dresden Gallery in Germany, and more than forty other museums throughout the previous Soviet Union. Works by Fomin are in private collections in Belgium, Finland, France, Italy, Japan, Switzerland, and the United States. Finley Collection artist Nikita Fomin is his son.

At the Bridge, *1993.*
Oil on canvas.
21¾ x 16 inches.

ALEKſEI IVANOV

(1955 –)

Aleksei Ivanov was born in 1955 in St. Petersburg. He graduated from the Repin Institute and is now a painting teacher at the Berzen State Pedagogical University. He is also a member of the Russian Artists' Union.

Ivanov has many interests, which include landscape, portrait, and genre painting. He has painted a series of landscapes depicting modern life in France, where his daughter lives, and also a series of St. Petersburg landscapes. His palette is limited to a few hues, and he has been particularly influenced by the Post-Impressionist movement, especially Cézanne, and by Marquet, Sisley, and Bonnard.

Ivanov's works have been exhibited widely.

Portrait of an Old Man, *1996.*
Oil on canvas.
15 ⅛ x 15 ⅛ inches.

YURA KALYUTA

(1957 –   )

Yura Kalyuta was born in the
Ukrainian town of Krivoi Rog
(Bent Horn) in 1957. Kalyuta studied from 1983 to 1989 at the Repin
Institute under Andrei Mylnikov.
Student work by Kalyuta from his
fifth year at the Repin stands in the
Science and Research Museum at
the Academy of Arts, Russia. He
created his diploma work, *City of
Peter,* as a monumental stained glass
for the Hotel Saint Petersburg. The
National Academy of Arts included
Kalyuta's diploma in a national
exhibit of the best diploma works
from all institutions of higher education. In 1989 Kalyuta received the
postgraduate position of *aspirantura*
under Mylnikov. With this position
the artist is awarded a studio and is
expected to eventually become a
teacher at an Academy of Arts
Institution. Kalyuta has taught
drawing on the architectural faculty
of the Repin, painting to first-year
students, and currently teaches
drawing in the second-year painting
studio of Pimenov. The Artists'
Union accepted Kalyuta in 1991,
and he serves on the Painters'
Section Bureau.

Kalyuta paints landscapes and still
lifes, and his narrative compositions

Wife in a Turban,
1989. Sepia on paper.
28¾ x 14⅞ inches.

RIGHT:
Haircut in the Red
Studio, *1997.*
Oil on canvas.
59¹⁄₁₆ x 47⅝ inches.

65

use only subject matter inspired by his family.

Kalyuta exhibits regularly in St. Petersburg, Moscow, Hamburg, and Berlin. His works are in private collections in Bulgaria, England, France, Germany, Russia, and the United States. In 1997 his work was featured in the Beijing Art Museum, Beijing, China. His painting *Melissa* hangs in its permanent collection.

I Went Out for a
Walk with the Dog,
1997. Oil on canvas.
55¼ x 63⅛ inches.

MARINA GENADIEVNA KRAKAEVA

(1957–)

Marina Genadievna Krakaeva was born in Zabaikalie in 1957 and graduated from the art school in Ryazan. She studied graphic arts at the Academy of Industrial Arts in St. Petersburg and now teaches graphic arts at an art college.

Since 1993 Krakaeva has participated in all Voronezh art exhibitions. Living in Voronezh, Krakaeva also designs books for the Central-Chernozem publishing house.

Summer, *No Date.*
Oil on canvas. 17^{13}⁄$_{16}$ x 20^{1}⁄$_{16}$ inches.

RIGHT:
Detail of Summer.

ALEXANDER KREMER

(1958 –)

Alexander Kremer was born in St. Petersburg in 1958. He is a graduate of the Academy of Industrial Arts in St. Petersburg, Russia. From his father and grandfather, both artists, he has developed a strong love of Russian landscape. Kremer is most widely known for his "snow paintings," and he prefers the warm light and long, blue shadows of early sunset.

A prolific painter, Kremer exhibits regularly in Russia and Europe. He lives with his family in St. Petersburg.

BELOW:
Birches, *No Date.*
Oil on canvas.
16⅛ x 19½ inches.

RIGHT:
In the Park, *No Date.*
Oil on canvas.
23¹¹⁄₁₆ x 27⅝ inches.

ARSEN H. KURBANOV

(1969 –)

Arsen H. Kurbanov was born in Makhachkala, Dagestan, in 1969 to artist parents. In 1988 he finished the Jamal Dagestan Art College, receiving a red diploma, which signifies scholastic excellence. Kurbanov was immediately accepted at the Repin Institute in St. Petersburg, where he studied with the late Neprintsov. He graduated from the Repin in 1994.

Kurbanov strives to combine the techniques of the old masters — Pieter de Hooch and Vermeer are two of his favorites — with a contemporary, personal sense of imagery. Biblical and historical references appear alongside modern elements in his paintings, often producing an atmosphere of mystery. Portraiture commands a prominent position in his work. His portraits are intended to be compositions in their own right, in addition to presenting precise, almost photographic likenesses of the sitters.

Since graduation Kurbanov has been painting in Russia and abroad. In 1993, the St. Petersburg House of Cinema featured his work in a solo exhibition. He has participated in Artists' Union exhibitions in Moscow, St. Petersburg, and Makhachkala. Twice Kurbanov has exhibited his work in the German cities of Hamburg and Berlin. In 1997 he won the exhibition/ competition *My Russia . . . My World,* at the United Nations informational center in Moscow.

Kurbanov lives in St. Petersburg. Finley Collection artist Yaroslav Kurbanov is his brother.

BELOW:
Portrait of Masha,
1994–1995.
Oil on canvas.
18 x 15⅞ inches.

OPPOSITE:
Detail of Portrait of Masha.

YAROSLAV KURBANOV

(1968 –)

Yaroslav Kurbanov was born in Makhachkala, Dagestan, in 1968 to artist parents. After finishing the Jamal Dagestan Art College in Makhachkala in 1987 and serving his term in the army, Kurbanov studied painting and theater from 1990 to 1996 at the Repin Institute under the artist Eduard Kachirgin, artistic director of St. Petersburg's famous Big Dramatic Theater. A student in the Repin's theatrical program, he studied painting just as all other painting students do, but in addition had six years of courses in set and costume design.

The Renaissance is one of the most powerful influences on this artist, especially the work of Botticelli and Leonardo da Vinci. Kurbanov's work also reflects his experience copying the Flemish masters at St. Petersburg's Hermitage museum.

His work has traveled to Germany, France, Italy, Belgium, and the United States. During the summer of 1997, the American Consulate in St. Petersburg presented a solo exhibition of Kurbanov's work. His paintings are in diverse institutional and private collections around the world, including the permanent collection of the city of Genoa, Italy, and the collection of the former American Consul in St. Petersburg. Now graduated, he lives in St. Petersburg painting and exhibiting. Finley Collection artist Arsen Kurbanov is his brother.

Artist and the Muse, *1992. Oil on canvas. 38 ½ x 38 inches.*

OPPOSITE:
Detail of Artist and the Muse.

Female Nude, *1996.*
Oil on canvas.
29⁷⁄₁₆ x 29⁷⁄₁₆ inches.

Young Girl's Profile,
1997. Oil on canvas.
11⅛ x 11⅛ inches.

ALEXANDER KURZANOV

(1938–)

Alexander Kurzanov was born in Voronezh in 1938 and studied painting at Moscow University of Art from 1957 to 1960. He continued his studies from 1960 to 1965 in Ryazan and in 1972 he graduated from the Academy of Art in Tbilisi, Georgia.

Although he paints striking landscapes of the Voronezh region where he lives, he is also known for historical and political paintings as well as portraits of elderly people.

Since 1973, Kurzanov has participated in regional, republic, and national exhibitions. He has exhibited in Czechoslovakia, England, France, Germany, and Spain and his paintings are in the collections of the Russian Ministry of Culture, the Russian Artists' Union, and museums of art in several Russian cities. Numerous portraits and still lifes by Kurzanov are in the Voronezh Kramskoi Museum of Art.

ABOVE:
Tatiana Dmitrievna Vasileva Crocheting, 1967. *Oil on canvas. 47 x 30¾₆ inches.*

BELOW:
Popova in the Cobalt Factory, *No Date. Oil on canvas. 50⅞₆ x 34¼ inches.*

OPPOSITE:
The Frozen Garden, 1980. *Oil on canvas. 35⅞₆ x 23¼ inches.*

KURZANOV

BORIS V. LESOV

(1945 –   )

Boris V. Lesov was born in 1945 on Solovki Island, north of St. Petersburg. He studied at a St. Petersburg art school for children, and subsequently finished art college in the same city. In 1971 he graduated from Andrei Mylnikov's mural painting studio at the Repin Institute, then completed two years of postgraduate work under Mylnikov. Soon after graduation he became a member of the Artists' Union. Lesov has taught painting and drawing at college level for over ten years.

A strong influence on this artist has been the extensive travel opportunities provided by the Artists' Union. This allowed him to paint terrain from Habarovsk to Vladivostock, which included Siberian tundra, forests, volcanos and seashore.

Lesov creates both public artwork and easel paintings. He has painted more than forty public pieces, including murals at the Chernyshevshy Museum in Saratov. Other works can be seen in most major cities in Russia, as well as many European countries and the United States. Lesov lives in St. Petersburg with his family.

ABOVE:
Grasses and Flowers, *1993. Oil on canvas. 45 x 47⅛ inches.*

BELOW:
Fields, *1994. Oil on canvas. 23¹⁵⁄₁₆ x 25⅛ inches.*

OPPOSITE:
Detail of Grasses and Flowers.

MIKHAIL IVANOVICH LIKHACHEV

(1919–1997)

Mikhail Ivanovich Likhachev, an Honored Artist of Russia, was born near Voronezh in 1919. His first steps toward art were taken via the Voronezh Theater while preparing for his studies at the Voronezh Art College. After returning from serving in the Red Army during World War II, Likhachev went to Moscow to study in the studio of Boris Ioganson. After returning to Voronezh, Likhachev participated in all regional and national exhibits of the Artists' Union.

Likhachev painted historical compositions and portraits of ordinary people. He witnessed most of the political changes of this century in Russia, and the resulting historical artworks, many of them about World War II, are in museums throughout Russia. The Finley Collection has a fine sampling of his portrait studies, which include a wide variety of subjects — young ladies in colorful smocks and stocky peasants in their tired work clothes.

Likhachev was a tremendous force among the artists of Voronezh, and popular throughout Russia, evidenced by the fact that V. A. Gorchakov believes he may be the only artist to receive the award "Honored Artist of Russia" without having graduated from an art institute. Artworks by Likhachev are in the former Soviet Union's state collection and the permanent collection of the Russian Ministry of Culture, as well as numerous private collections in Russia and around the world.

ABOVE:
From Cabin to
Cabin, *1989.*
Oil on canvas.
31 7/16 x 35 1/2 inches.

OPPOSITE:
The Two, *1986.*
Oil on canvas.
39 11/16 x 27 1/4 inches.

OVERLEAF:
Detail of From Cabin
to Cabin.

83

Galya, *1966.*
Oil on gessoed carton.
22½ x 13¼ inches.

Young Woman in
Red, *1956.*
Oil on gessoed carton.
13 x 10 inches.

OPPOSITE:

In the Sun, *1951.*
Oil on gessoed carton.
13½ x 10¼ inches.

Female Worker, *1960.*
Oil on gessoed carton.
15⅛ x 12³⁄₁₆ inches.

TOP RIGHT:
The Beet Picker, *1968.*
Oil on gessoed carton.
19¼ x 13½ inches.

BOTTOM RIGHT:
Study of a Woman in
Red, *1960.*
Oil on gessoed carton.
16½ x 12 inches.

OPPOSITE:
Shepherd, *1972 or*
1970. Oil on gessoed
carton. 18¼ x 13¾ inches.

Woman with Chin on
Her Hands, *No Date.*
Graphite on paper.
12½ x 15⅞ inches.

OPPOSITE:
Detail of Woman with
Chin on Her Hands.

ABOVE:
Laughing Girl in
Scarf, *No Date.*
Graphite on paper.
10½ x 7½ inches.

LEFT:
Schoolgirl in Braids,
No Date.
Graphite on paper.
10½ x 7½ inches.

Wife, 1946.
Graphite on paper.
15⅞ x 11¼ inches.

TOP LEFT:

Woman Doing
Needlepoint, *1954.*
Graphite on paper.
10⅛ x 7½ inches.

BOTTOM LEFT:

Artist's Wife, *1956.*
Black and sienna
conté stick.
11¾ x 8⅛ inches.

TOP RIGHT:

Female Face,
No Date.
Graphite on paper.
15⅞ x 11⅛ inches.

BOTTOM RIGHT:

Woman Reading,
No Date.
Charcoal on paper.
10⅛ x 7½ inches.

TOP LEFT:
Portrait of an Old
Woman (Front),
1950. Graphite on paper.
14⅞ x 11⅛ inches.

BOTTOM LEFT:
Elderly Woman at
Window, *1948.*
Graphite on paper.
14⅞ x 11⅛ inches.

TOP RIGHT:
Portrait of an Old
Woman (Back), *1950.*
Graphite on paper.
14⅞ x 11⅛ inches.

BOTTOM RIGHT:
Elderly Woman,
1953. Graphite on
paper.
7½ x 5⅛ inches.

OPPOSITE:
Elderly Woman
Seated near Bed,
1949. Ink wash on
paper. 14⅞ x 11 inches.

TOP LEFT:
Seated Boy, *No Date.*
Mixed media.
10⅛ x 7½ inches.

BOTTOM LEFT:
A Boy's Face, II, *No*
Date. Graphite on paper.
10⅛ x 7½ inches.

TOP RIGHT:
A Boy's Face, *No Date.*
Graphite on paper.
10⅛ x 7½ inches.

BOTTOM RIGHT:
A Boy's Face with
Shadow, *No Date.*
Graphite on paper.
9½ x 8⅛ inches.

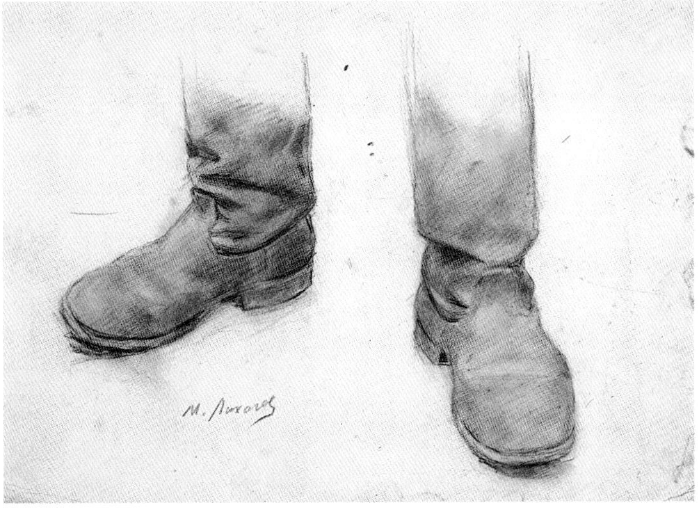

TOP LEFT:

Young Man Sketching, *1954. Graphite on paper. 10 5/8 x 7 3/8 inches.*

BOTTOM LEFT:

Old Man with Mustache, *1954. Graphite on paper. 10 5/8 x 7 1/2 inches.*

ABOVE:

Man's Portrait, *No Date. Graphite on paper. 14 5/8 x 11 1/8 inches.*

BELOW:

Boots, *No Date. Charcoal on paper. 11 3/8 x 15 3/8 inches.*

OVERLEAF:

Detail of Boots.

М. Лихачёв

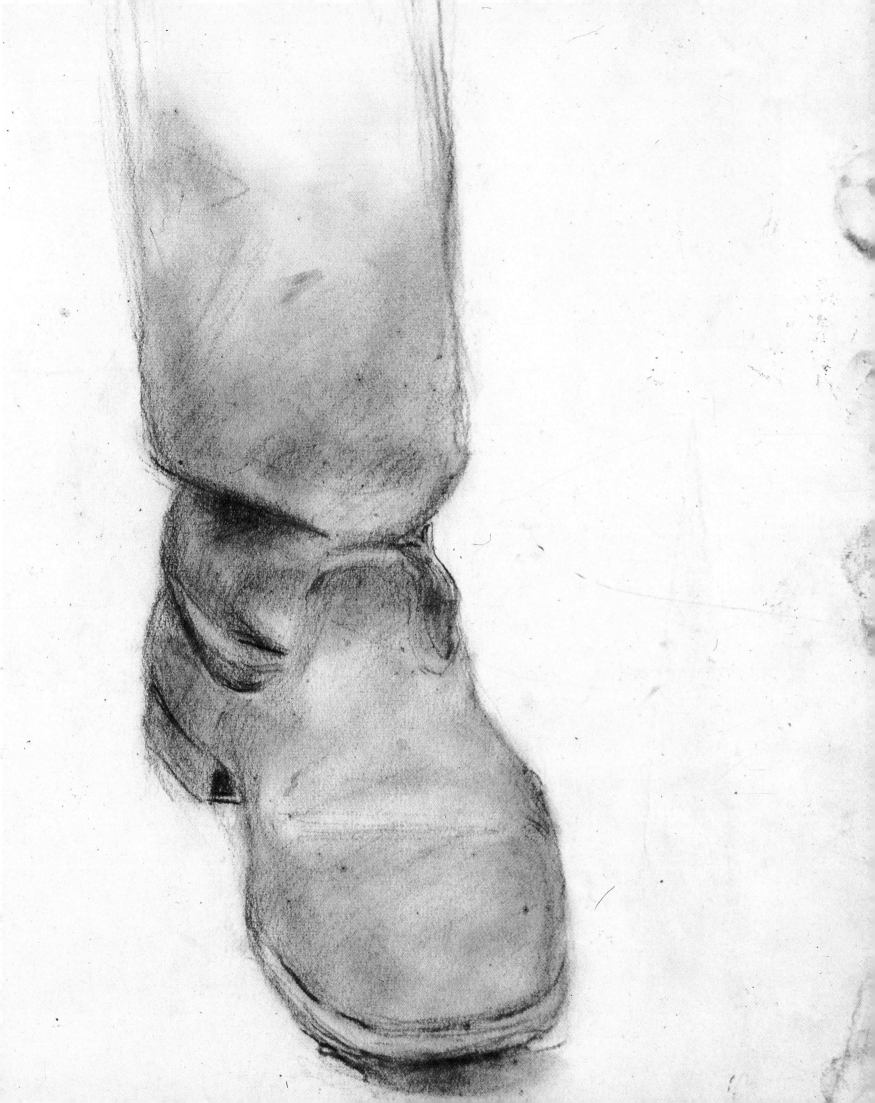

VALENTIN MAKHITARIANTS

(1943 –)

Valentin Makhitariants was born in the Northern Caucasus city of Vladikavkaz in 1943, and graduated from Andrei Mylnikov's mural painting studio at the Repin Institute in 1975.

Makhitariants paints with soft colors and uses textured surfaces, and his figures are somewhat stylized. The Makhitariants painting in the Finley Collection is a *postanovka* from his student days. A *postanovka* is a unified stage composed of the background draperies and props against which a model is posed for painting.

From his St. Petersburg studio, Makhitariants works on easel paintings and monumental artworks. He has been active in national and international exhibits for over twenty years. His works are in museums and private collections in Finland, France, Greece, Italy, Russia, Spain, and Sweden.

Female Nude on Green Background, *1972. Oil on canvas. 39¼ x 31⁷⁄₁₆ inches.*

OPPOSITE:
Detail of Female Nude on Green Background.

ANDREI ANDREEVICH MYLNIKOV

(1919–)

Andrei Andreevich Mylnikov was born in Pokrovsk in 1919. He entered the Repin Institute as a student of architecture, but later switched to the mural painting studio of Igor Grabar. Mylnikov's 1946 diploma painting, *Baltic Sailors' Oath*, earned him a master's degree, and established him as a major power in the St. Petersburg art world. In 1946 he was awarded an *aspirantura* postgraduate studio, and by 1947 he was already on the teaching staff of the Repin. During the 1948–49 academic year, Mylnikov assumed command of the mural painting studio. He was the youngest artist to be assigned this responsibility. In 1953 the role of directing the painting department of the Repin was added to his duties. In 1963 Mylnikov was awarded the position as head of the professional studio of mural painting of the St. Petersburg Academy of Arts.

Mylnikov has mastered almost all traditional, two-dimensional media. He paints vital landscapes around Russia and the world. Portraits, still lifes, nudes, and decorative themes are created in abundance by this artist, who also sculpts. He is perhaps most widely known for his work as a mural artist and as head of the studio of mural painting at the Repin. (In Russia, the mural painting studio is known as the monumental painting studio— monumental referring not so much to scale as to methods and materials appropriate for public spaces such as stained glass, tapestry, fresco and sgraffito.)

In 1951 Mylnikov received the State Laureate Prize of the USSR for his painting *On Peaceful Fields*. In 1957 he achieved the title of professor. His painting *Parting* earned him another State Laureate Prize in 1977. In 1979 his work as head of the team that created the mosaics in the halls of the memorial complex for the heroes who defended Leningrad during World War II earned him a third State Laureate Prize. In 1981 the Academy of Arts of the USSR awarded Mylnikov a gold medal for his triptych *Crucifixion*. He received the award of Lenin in 1984 for the same triptych. Mylnikov is an Honored Artist of Russia, and has been a member of the Leningrad Cultural Fund. He has served as a deputy in the Soviet Government.

It is difficult to imagine how the "aboveground" art world of St. Petersburg would look today without the influence of academician Andrei Mylnikov. He has taught fifty-one years and has been a creative rudder for the painting department of the Repin Institute for forty-eight years. Mylnikov has been involved in the initiation of cultural programs, public monuments, the restoration of churches, and even the restoration of the Hermitage's vandalized *Danae*, by Rembrandt.

Untitled, 1996.
Oil on canvas.
23¹³⁄₁₆ x 18⅛ inches.

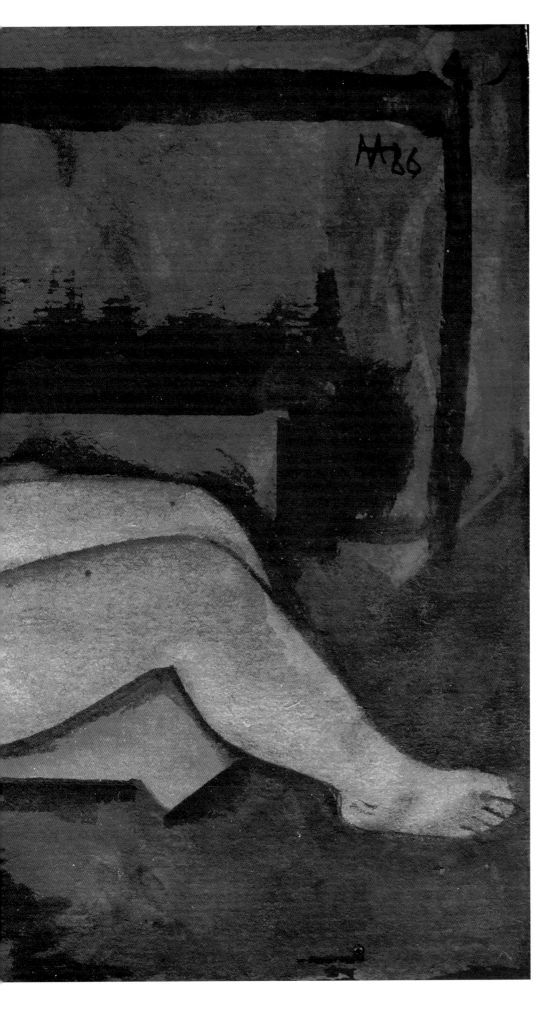

Works by Mylnikov are in most museums around the former Soviet Union, including the State Russian Museum in St. Petersburg and the Tretyakov Gallery in Moscow. Mylnikov is well represented in several major collections in Asia. Between 1946 and 1978 alone, he was in over seventy exhibitions. His monumental compositions adorn metro stations and public buildings across Russia. At least three books have been published about the artist's work.

Although battling illness, Mylnikov continues to paint and teach in St. Petersburg with undiminished intensity. His daughter, son-in-law, and granddaughter are artists. His wife, Aria, a former prima ballerina, teaches ballet.

Untitled, 1986.
*Watercolor and gouache on
paper. 7⅜ x 11 inches.*

Untitled, 1985.
Oil on panel.
20¼ x 22⅞ inches.

Lilacs in the White
Nights, *1990.*
Oil on canvas.
39¼ x 39¼ inches.

Green Island, *1977.*
Oil on canvas.
39³⁄₁₆ x 39³⁄₁₆ inches.

OPPOSITE:
Detail of Green Island.

ANATOLY ALEXEEVICH NEBOLSIN

(1934–)

Anatoly Alexeevich Nebolsin was born in Gorenskiye Vyselki Village, in the Voronezh region in 1934. In 1965 Nebolsin received his master's degree in painting at the Tashkent Art Institute in Uzbekistan, but he has lived in Voronezh for most of his life.

Nebolsin paints landscape and figure compositions featuring traditional Russian culture. His specialty is seascapes; he travels to the coast for two to three months each year where he does many studies, which serve as references for works to be painted in the studio.

In the past, Nebolsin taught at the Voronezh Art College, but he now concentrates solely on painting and exhibiting. He regularly participates in national, regional, and local exhibitions, as well as exhibits in Warsaw, Poland.

Autumn Chores,
1996. Oil on canvas.
30 1/16 x 31 9/16 inches.

ABOVE:
Fall Days, *1982.*
Oil on canvas.
23 11/16 x 26 inches.

Young Milkmaids,
1963. Oil on canvas.
40⅞ x 23¼ inches.

OVERLEAF:
Detail of Young
Milkmaids.

Picking Mushrooms,
1978. Oil on canvas.
31³⁄₁₆ x 62¼ inches.

OLEG POMERANTSEV

(1949–)

Oleg Pomerantsev was born in 1949 in Chelyabinsk, a small town in the heart of the Ural Mountains. At the age of 17, he left the Urals and began his education at Leningrad's Engineering and Architectural College. He graduated in 1972 as a certified architect and then began his professional career in nuclear plant building. He designed two of the largest nuclear plant buildings in Russia and in 1978 he was accepted as a member of the Guild of Architects of the USSR.

His childhood experience of life in the Urals had provided him with a view of the authentic Russian landscape, but Pomerantsev did not begin to paint that imagery until the 1980s. In addition to painting, Pomerantsev studied graphics and also mastered the technique of watercolor.

Pomerantsev's art is represented in numerous galleries in St. Petersburg and around the world. He has had shows and exhibits in Europe and the United States and his works are in private collections and art galleries in more than twenty countries.

The Storm, *No Date.*
Watercolor on paper.
7 x 7¼ inches.

ABOVE:
Untitled, *1994.*
Watercolor on paper.
11½ x 14 inches.

OPPOSITE:
Saturday, *1994.*
Watercolor on paper.
5⅛ x 7⅛ inches.

Ships in the St.
Petersburg Harbor,
1996. Oil on canvas.
21¼ x 25⅝ inches.

VLADIMIR VICTOROVICH PROJHKIN

(1931–)

Vladimir Victorovich Proshkin was born in St. Petersburg in 1931 to artist parents. When the Germans encircled Leningrad during World War II, Proshkin's parents sent him to Siberia for three years. Although he considers St. Petersburg home, the artist believes that his time spent in the Siberian wilderness molded him into a landscape painter. When Proshkin returned to St. Petersburg, he attended the Middle Art School, then was accepted into the Repin Institute, where he studied under Boris Ioganson. Proshkin attests that he stood out from his fellow students because he usually managed to fulfill the weekly composition assignments using landscape. It naturally followed that in 1957 the theme of his diploma paintings should be landscape. Since graduation, Proshkin's career has remained focused on the same genre.

A member of the Artists' Union since 1958, he has participated in almost all exhibits open to St. Petersburg artists, including city-wide, regional, state, and national exhibits. He serves in the St. Petersburg Artists' Union's Bureau of Painters. He has shown his work in Germany, Italy, Japan, and the United States. Solo exhibits of Proshkin's work have taken place in St. Petersburg, Moscow, Pskov, Pechorah, Izborsk, and Elgav.

Many museums throughout the former Soviet Union possess paintings by Proshkin, including the State Russian Museum, the National Pushkin Museum, the Museum of the History of St. Petersburg, the Museum of the Summer Garden, the Omsk Art Gallery, and the Krasnoyarsk Art Museum. Proshkin and his wife, who works at the Manezh exhibition hall, live in St. Petersburg in a historic studio and flat which belonged to Proshkin's parents. The couple spends summers painting and gardening at their dacha in Latvia.

At the Edge of Aksenev, 1996. Oil on canvas. 26 x 35 ⁷⁄₁₆ inches.

NIKOLAI NIKITAVICH REPIN

(1932 –   )

Nikolai Nikitavich Repin was born in the Kursk region of Russia in 1932. Repin has been a resident of St. Petersburg since completing his studies, first at the Leningrad Pedagogical Art College in 1956, then at the Repin Institute in the mural painting studio under Andrei Mylnikov. While still doing post-graduate work at the Institute, Repin was invited by the artist Boris Ugarov, then rector of the Academy, to teach in his studio, where they then worked together for many years.

Repin's works are primarily land-scapes of northern Russia and por-traiture. The painting of the artist's daughter, *Natasha on the Veranda* (above right), has won awards at shows hosted by the Russian Artists' Union, of which Repin is a member.

Paintings by Nikolai Repin are in the permanent collections of the Museum of the Academy of Art in St. Petersburg, the Aivazovsky Museum in Feodosia, the Direction Museum in St. Petersburg, the Museum of the History of St. Petersburg, the Museum of Art in Joshkar-Ola, and the Dracon Museum of Art in Taiwan. The cities of St. Petersburg, Kranstadt, and Milan have hosted one-man shows of Repin's work.

Natasha on the Veranda, *1995.*
Oil on canvas.
23⅛ x 29⅛ inches.

OPPOSITE:
Detail of Natasha on the Veranda.

With Victory, *1995.*
Oil on canvas.
59 x 58⅛ inches.

OVERLEAF:
Detail of With Victory.

NATALIA NIKOLAEVNA REPINA

(1967 –)

Natalia Nikolaevna Repina was born in 1967 in St. Petersburg, where she studied at the Middle Art School from 1979 until 1985. She studied painting at the Repin Institute from 1985 until 1991, graduating from the studio of Boris Ugarov. Repina now lives and works in St. Petersburg, and is a member of the Russian Artists' Union. In 1996 she completed a special skills course, *stazherovka,* in the architectural department of the Repin Institute. Since 1991 Repina has been teaching drawing at the Architectural Construction Institute in St. Petersburg.

Repina paints still lifes and interiors, as well as landscapes from the St. Petersburg and Crimea areas. She favors loose brushwork and naturalistic color. Works by Repina are in the Scientific Research Museum of the Academy of Arts, and in the Dostoyevsky Museum, both in St. Petersburg. Her paintings and drawings are also in private collections in Finland, France, Germany, Russia, and the United States.

Repina's paintings were included in a group show of student work from the Repin, which traveled to the New York Academy and to Glasgow from 1988 to 1989. Since 1991 she has regularly participated in all annual Russian Artists' Union exhibits. From 1994 to 1997 she participated in French auctions at the Arkol gallery. An exhibit of Repina's work took place at the Dostoyevsky Museum in St. Petersburg in 1996. Repina's works have also been exhibited at the Shanghai Museum in China. Finley Collection artist Nikolai Repin is her father.

Crimean Street, *No Date. Oil on canvas. 16 x 14¼ inches.*

VERONICA REPKINA

(1966 –)

Veronica Repkina was born in St. Petersburg in 1966. She completed the Middle Art School and after graduating with highest marks in 1994 from Andrei Mylnikov's mural painting studio at the Repin Institute, Repkina was given the honor of a postgraduate creative studio.

Repkina is best known for her landscapes and portraits. Her work has been influenced by the Renaissance movement and World of Art movement and is characterized by the refined lines and subtle treatment of light and shade found in the paintings of Raphael and Botticelli. Repkina admires the Russian artists Benois, Bakst, Borisov-Musatov, and Samov.

St. Petersburg, Russia, is the home of Repkina, her husband Boris Bobkin, a Repin graduate, and their sons.

Yellow Still Life,
1993. Oil on canvas.
35 x 38½ inches.

OPPOSITE:
Detail of Yellow
Still Life.

C. Zervos

Picasso

Paris

GALINA RUMYANTSEVA

(1927–   )

Born in St. Petersburg in 1927, Galina Rumyantseva graduated from the Repin Institute in 1957. She studied under Boris Ioganson and is a member of the St. Petersburg Artists' Union.

Since graduation, her paintings have been acquired by several Russian museums, including the Kuntskamera, the Museum of Ethnography, and Perm Kraznodar.

She has also exhibited in France, Holland, Germany, Switzerland, and the United Kingdom.

Morning Milking,
1952. Oil on board.
9⅛ x 14 inches.

IRINA NIKOLAEVNA SAFRANOVA

(1950 –)

Irina Nikolaevna Safranova was born in Moscow in 1950. She earned her master's degree in dress design in St. Petersburg at the Academy of Industrial Arts in 1972, after which she worked at the Leningrad House of Dress Modeling. Today Safranova is the head of the department for clothing design at the St. Petersburg State University of Technology and Design. She lectures part-time on costume design at the Repin Institute's theatrical department, and is a costume designer at the St. Petersburg Maly Opera and Ballet Theater.

Safranova creates spirited, colorful water-media paintings, which serve as her portfolio in the professional world.

Safranova's designs and paintings have been exhibited and collected in Europe and the United States. She is married to Finley Collection artist Nikita Fomin.

In Disguise, *1995.*
Mixed water media on
prepared paper.
24 x 19½ inches.

134

Doll Theater, *1995.*
Mixed water media on
prepared paper.
20 x 23 inches.

OPPOSITE:
County Fair, *1995.*
Mixed water media on
prepared paper.
24 ⅛ x 19 ½ inches.

YURI PETROVICH SANIN

(1938 –)

Yuri Petrovich Sanin was born in Voronezh in 1938 and received his artistic training at the Minsk Art College in Penza (south of Moscow).

Early in his career, Sanin was heavily influenced by the French Impressionists. As his career progressed, he was influenced by the Russian itinerant painters who were active during the last half of the nineteenth century and the early part of the twentieth century until the revolution. Their favorite theme was peasant life. Other artists who have influenced Sanin include the Russian landscape painters Shishkin and Kramskoi. (Kramskoi is from the Voronezh region and the Voronezh art museum is named for him.) Sanin's relationship to naturalistic realism has been a constant throughout his career.

Since 1966 Sanin has been in regional and national exhibitions. He is a member of the Russian Artists' Union and although Voronezh is his home base, Sanin frequently travels in order to paint a variety of landscapes.

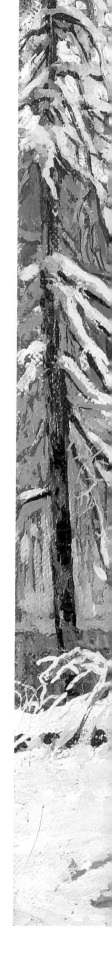

Snowy Winter, *1993.*
Oil on canvas.
18⅛ x 18⅛ inches.

BELOW:
Suburbs, *1975.*
Oil on canvas.
35⅛ x 51½₆ inches.

OPPOSITE:

In a Birch Forest,
1966. Oil on canvas.
33 x 18⅛ inches.

ABOVE:

Grasses at the
House, *1983.*
Oil on canvas.
31⅜ x 31⁷⁄₁₆ inches.

LEFT:

The Village of
Mepovatka, *1976.*
Oil on canvas.
23¹³⁄₁₆ x 31⅜ inches.

OVERLEAF:

Detail of The Village
of Mepovatka.

Summer in Duhovoye,
1986. Oil on canvas.
31 11/16 x 35 7/16 inches.

Evening, *1965.*
Oil on canvas.
17 ³⁄₁₆ x 27 ³⁄₁₆ inches.

VLADIMIR I. SHEDRIN

(1942 –   )

Vladimir I. Shedrin was born in
Voronezh in 1942 and educated in
the town of Penza.

Shedrin is primarily a landscape
painter, and for many years the
theme of his paintings was "our
town." The Finley Collection has
several examples of these paintings,
which are characterized by brilliant,
vibrant color applied in broad
brushstrokes. They also feature
unusual points of view; rather than
presenting a limited view of the village from a pedestrian's eye-level,
Shedrin paints the entire village in
bird's-eye perspective. Another of
Shedrin's themes is "at the dacha."
Every year he goes to the Academic
Dacha in the countryside outside of
Moscow, where he paints for two or
three months. Shedrin's dacha
paintings tend to be more naturalistic and use local color.

Shedrin has exhibited in France,
Germany, and the United States as
well as his native Russia. He lives
in Voronezh.

Birches in the
Spring, *1990.*
Oil on canvas.
33 ⁷⁄₁₆ x 29 ⅛ inches.

Awakening, *1992.*
Oil on canvas.
25 ⅛ x 29 ⅛ inches.

RIGHT:
Village in the Fall,
1967. Oil on canvas.
35 ⅛ x 39 ½ inches.

147

The South-West
Region, *1969.*
Oil on canvas.
31 7/16 x 49 1/2 inches.

Fall in the Village,
1968. Oil on canvas.
35 ⅛ x 51 ¹¹/₁₆ inches.

150

The Old Market,
1968. Oil on canvas.
47⅜ x 43⅜ inches.

RIGHT:
Portrait of the
Artist's Daughter,
1966. Oil on panel.
27⅝ x 19½ inches.

Village Festival, *1972.*
Oil on canvas.
38⁵⁄₁₆ x 49⁷⁄₁₆ inches.

VLADIMIR YEVGENEVICH SHPAKOVSKY

(1950 –   )

Vladimir Yevgenevich Shpakovsky was born in Kursk in 1950. He received his master's degree from the artistic-graphic department of the Kursk State Teaching Institute, where he simultaneously taught drawing. From 1972 to 1980 he taught drawing and painting at the Buturlinov Artistic-Graphic College and from 1980 to 1994 he taught at the Voronezh Art College. Shpakovsky has been the dean of the painting department of the Voronezh State Institute of Art since 1994.

Shpakovsky's paintings include narrative compositions, portraits, and landscapes and have been exhibited several times annually in Moscow and Voronezh since 1977. In 1993 his paintings traveled to Frankfurt with the exhibit *Artists of Voronezh* and in 1996 the University

Dvoryanskaya Street (Palace Street), *1992. Oil on canvas. 20³⁄₁₆ x 23¾ inches.*

of Tennessee at Chattanooga
invited Shpakovsky to be an artist
in residence. The resulting show
and lectures were enthusiastically
received; two large oils of his
remain in the university's permanent collection. A relationship
between Shpakovsky and the organization Art Teaches the World
enabled the teacher in 1996 to bring
four of his students to the United
States for one month of painting
landscapes.

Works by Shpakovsky have been
featured in the Artists' Union jour-
nal *Artist* and are in the Voronezh
Kramskoi Museum of Art, the
Offices of the Director of Artistic
Exhibits of Russia, the Ryazan
Gallery in Russia, the Frankfurt on
Main Gallery in Germany, and
many private collections in
Germany and the United States.

The Cow Barn, *1984.*
Oil on canvas.
47½ x 59½ inches.

158

The Song, *1995.*
Oil on canvas.
30½ x 40⅛ inches.

ALEXEI KONSTANTINOVICH SOKOLOV

(1922 –   )

Alexei Konstantinovich Sokolov was born in St. Petersburg in 1922 into a family of artists, writers, and theater professionals. From the age of eight he studied drawing and painting at the Lilian Studio in St. Petersburg. Until 1938 he studied at the Palace of Pioneers (Anitchkov Palace), where teachers from the Repin taught gifted youths. Sokolov attended the Academy of Arts' Middle Art School from 1938 until 1941, at which time he went to war as a volunteer in the National Guard. In 1944, the Repin Institute accepted Sokolov without examinations. In his third year he entered the mural painting studio of Igor Grabar in order to study with Andrei Mylnikov, who also taught in Grabar's studio. In 1951 graduate Sokolov was offered an *aspirantura* position, which he occupied until the opportunity arose to move with the Mylnikovs into a double apartment with studios. Beginning in 1952 Sokolov taught painting and composition at the St. Petersburg Academy of Industrial Arts.

In 1960 Sokolov spent two years in France and this proved a very fertile period for him. He

Party Bouquet, *1995.*
Oil on canvas.
38 ¹³⁄₁₆ x 41 ³⁄₁₆ inches.

OPPOSITE:
Still Life with Three Vases, *1995.*
Oil on canvas.
35 ⁷⁄₁₆ x 27 ⅞ inches.

befriended Russian artists A. A. Denyneka and Serebryakova, and the actress Marina Vladi. He fell in love with jazz, going to concerts of Louis Armstrong and Edith Piaf. He also met French writers and philosophers and attended theater before returning to Russia in late 1961.

In 1968, after being appointed studio head, Mylnikov invited Sokolov to join him in the mural painting studio at the Repin, where he still teaches today. From 1976 to 1983, Sokolov additionally served as dean of the Repin painting department.

Sokolov, an Honored Artist of Russia who holds the title of professor, exhibits regularly in many private exhibits and all Artists' Union exhibits. In 1960 he won grand prize in a juried exhibition at Paris's Grand Chalet for all young artists (native or foreign) working in France. Sokolov's paintings are in numerous Russian museums, including the State Russian Museum and the Theatrical Museum in St. Petersburg. He is represented in institutional and private collections in France, Germany, Russia and the United States.

Monumental works by Sokolov are numerous. *Peace to the World* (1956), a mosaic done together with Mylnikov, decorates St. Petersburg's metro station, Avtova. Other large pieces are in the Neva restaurant, the St. Petersburg Children's Theater, the Theater of Drama and Comedy, and the Moscow Na Taganke theater. Today Sokolov lives in St. Petersburg. He has a son, Leonid, also a Finley Collection artist, and two grandchildren.

Winter Canal, *1995.*
Oil on canvas.
21¼ x 28⁷⁄₁₆ inches.

LEONID ALEXEEVICH SOKOLOV

(1945–   )

Leonid Alexeevich Sokolov was
born in 1945 into a St. Petersburg
family with a long history in the
arts. His grandfather was one of the
founders of the St. Petersburg
Society of Encouragement of Artists
(now the Artists' Union). His father,
Alexei Sokolov, a Finley Collection
artist, is an outstanding painter with
works in major museums throughout
Russia and Europe. His mother is a
historian of theatrical arts. His wife,
Galina, is the art historian at the
Theatrical Museum of St. Petersburg, and Sokolov's son is studying
to be an artist.

Beginning in the ninth grade,
Sokolov studied at the art preparatory school no. 190. In 1971 he
received his master's degree as a
painter of porcelain and ceramics
from Mukhina, now called the Academy of Industrial Arts. Sokolov
spent the years from graduation
until 1990 fulfilling commissions
received through the Artists' Union
and Art Foundation. Since the
commissions dried up in 1990, he
has had to scale down, creating
glaze paintings on porcelain tiles,
vases, boxes, and one-of-a-kind tea
or coffee services with his unique
and frequently humorous motifs of

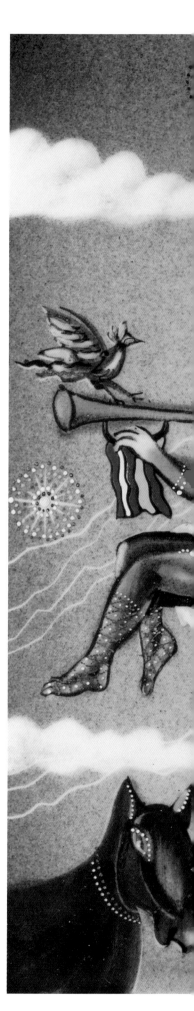

Dream Maker, *1995.*
Porcelain and glazes.
8 x 8 inches.

166

167

Untitled Porcelain
Tray I, *1996.*
Glazed porcelain.
10⅛ x 10⅛ inches.

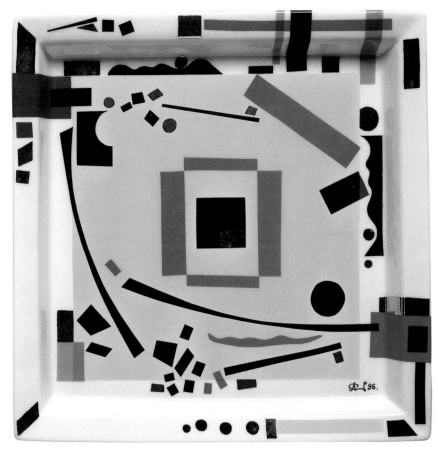

Untitled Porcelain
Tray II, *1996.*
Glazed porcelain.
10⅛ x 10⅛ inches.

circuses and carnivals. Sokolov's
technique combines high-fire
glazes, low-fire glazes, and the
application of gold.

Some of Sokolov's most popular
pieces are his glaze paintings on
porcelain eggs from the Lomono-
sov factory. Sokolov began painting
eggs with idyllic scenes of the
Russian countryside complete with
tiny chapels and priests. Soon experimentation began, however, and
today a Sokolov egg is as likely to
have a festive circus cavorting about
as it is to have a priest. Architectural
motifs from St. Petersburg have
appeared, wrapped around the egg
in a reverse panorama.

Sokolov has won numerous
prizes for modern porcelain,
including one in Germany which
earned him a trip to work at a
Frankfurt factory. He has twice
been artist in residence, teaching
and exhibiting, at Southern
Adventist University in Tennessee.
A one-man show featured Sokolov
in the winter of 1996–97 at the
Casino Conti in St. Petersburg. His
work is in collections across the
former Soviet Union and in the
United States, Germany, Canada,
and France.

VAJILY VLADIMIROVICH JUKHOV

(1949 –)

Vasily Vladimirovich Sukhov was born in St. Petersburg in 1949. Sukhov began his art studies in 1960 in the sixth grade at the Middle Arts School. Upon completing the Middle Arts School, he was accepted to the Repin Institute, where he studied with Andrei Mylnikov in the mural painting studio. From 1976 to 1980 Sukhov did postgraduate work, also under Mylnikov.

Sukhov is one of the four artists who, under the acronym FoRUS (Fomin, Repin, Uralov, and Sukhov), create monumental public works found all over St. Petersburg and Moscow, in restaurants, metro stations, hotels, and government buildings. Another FoRUS member, Nikita Fomin, is also represented in the Finley Collection.

Since 1972 Sukhov has participated in more than two hundred exhibits around the former Soviet Union. Sukhov is married and lives in St. Petersburg, teaching at the Middle Art School where he once studied.

Making Hay, *1994.*
Oil on canvas.
29½ x 31¼ inches.

OPPOJITE:
Detail of Making Hay.

KARL ALFREDOVITCH TANPETR

(1923–   )

Karl Alfredovitch Tanpetr was born in Gorky (now Nizhny-Novgorod) in 1923. He studied at the Kharkov Art Academy from which he graduated in 1955. He is a member of the Russian Artists' Union.

Milking Scene, *No Date. Oil on canvas. 18⅜ x 22⅞ inches.*

OPPOSITE:
Detail of Milking Scene.

ƧVETLANA ARKADYEVNA TERENTYEVA

(1948 –)

Ƨvetlana Arkadyevna Terentyeva was born in St. Petersburg in 1948. Despite the fact that her mother and grandfather were sculptors who hoped that she would continue their tradition, Terentyeva battled to become a musician, attending the musical preparatory school of the conservatory in St. Petersburg. Sculpture won out over music, however, and she was accepted at the Repin Institute in 1970. In 1976 her diploma sculpture, *Milkmaid,* earned her a degree with honors from the studio of the sculptor, Mikhail Anikushin, and she was immediately awarded a postgraduate creative studio.

During the Soviet period Terentyeva created monumental pieces, both for public sites and for exhibitions, but since monumental commissions have vanished she has been working on a more diminutive scale. Terentyeva prefers a corpulent model to a thin one. "They give you such a lush sense of form, and you get to really pile on the materials."

Terentyeva lives in St. Petersburg with her mother and her son.

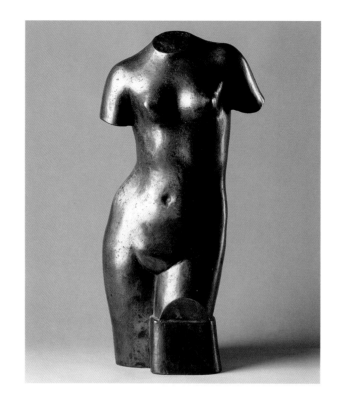

Standing Female
Nude Bronze
Figurine, *No Date.*
17 x 9 inches.

OPPOƧITE:
Detail of Standing
Female Nude Bronze
Figurine.

NIKOLAI ALEXEEVICH TRUNOV

(1924–   )

Nikolai Alexeevich Trunov was born in Nikolskoye Village in the Voronezh region in 1924. When he was sixteen years old, Trunov moved to Voronezh, where he began to visit museums and exhibits and to read art journals. By the age of seventeen, he was a student at the Voronezh Art College under Kolosov and Filosofov. When World War II began and the college was temporarily closed, Trunov went to the Zemliansk region, where he continued to pursue his career.

At one point during the war, Trunov lived in a city occupied by the Germans. On a particularly beautiful day he took some students out into the countryside to paint, where the group was ambushed and interrogated by German patrol soldiers. Upon producing paints, brushes, and field easels, the party convinced the Germans of their purpose and were released. The occupying Germans turned out to be art lovers, and encouraged the artists to paint wherever and whenever they wished. The German officers even bought some works from the artists.

Influenced heavily by the Impressionists, Trunov's portraits and landscapes exhibit the sensibil-

Winter Sunshine, 1965. Oil on canvas. 23 3/16 x 31 1/16 inches.

Pushkin Street, 1965.
Oil on canvas.
20 x 39⁹⁄₁₆ inches.

In My Garden, 1970.
Oil on canvas.
52¹¹⁄₁₆ x 45¼ inches.

Hollyhocks, *1960.*
Oil on canvas.
66¼ x 39¼ inches.

182

Row of Flowers,
1970. Oil on canvas.
35 ⅞ x 35 ¹³⁄₁₆ inches.

ity of a colorist. From childhood, he was more interested in color than in classical technique.

Trunov lives and paints in Voronezh, and is a member of the Voronezh chapter of the Russian Artists' Union. He exhibits frequently in Russia, and has several paintings in the Voronezh Kramskoi Museum of Art.

TOP:
Woman with
Gladiolias, *1960.*
Oil on canvas.
26 x 20¾ inches.

BOTTOM:
A Woman from
Kuban, *1957.*
Oil on canvas.
34 x 30¹⁵⁄₁₆ inches.

OPPOSITE:
Annushka, *1960.*
Oil on canvas.
16⅛ x 12¹⁄₁₆ inches.

GENADY VLADISLAVOVICH ULYBIN

(1973–)

Genady Vladislavovich Ulybin was born in Pervomeisk, Ukraine, in 1973. Before entering the Repin Institute, this Ukrainian artist finished the Kharkov State Art College in 1992. Ulybin studies easel painting in the painting studio of the late Neprintsov. He is one of the youngest artists in the Finley collection and will graduate from the Repin in 2000. He is a student member of the St. Petersburg chapter of the Russian Artists' Union.

Ulybin admires the Russian draftsman Chistyakov and the painters Repin and Serov. The Renaissance artists and Dutch masters are his main influences from the West. All genres and media interest Ulybin.

Paintings and drawings by Ulybin are in private collections in Russia, England, Germany, Italy, the United States, Poland, Afghanistan, and Finland.

Female Model, 1987.
Oil on canvas.
42⅛ x 29⅛ inches.

OPPOSITE:
Untitled Nude, 1990.
Oil on canvas.
31 x 38½ inches.

VYACHESLAV FRANTSEVICH ZAGONEK

(1919 – 1994)

Vyacheslav Frantsevich Zagonek was born in Irkustsk, Russia, in 1919, but lived in Czechoslovakia as a child. In 1927 his family returned to Russia, settling in St. Petersburg, where he lived for the remainder of his life.

Zagonek began painting and drawing in 1932 at a children's art school in St. Petersburg, and in 1936 was accepted as a fifth-year student at the Middle Art School of the Academy of Arts. World War II interrupted his studies in 1939; he served in the Red Army on the Leningrad Front until 1942, when he was released from active duty due to illness. After recovering, he worked on building campaigns in Murmansk and Archangel. In 1945 Zagonek was accepted to the Repin, where he studied under Boris Ioganson. His diploma painting was entitled *Spring on the Collective Farm* (1950).

Zagonek exhibited widely throughout his life and earned the title Honored Artist of Russia. His work is in museums across Russia and he was a correspondent member of the Russian Academy of Arts. His son, Vladimir, teaches at the Repin.

Spring Planting,
1949. Oil on canvas.
31⅜ x 45½ inches.

The Apple Pickers,
1979. Oil on canvas.
12⅞ x 25⅛ inches.

FYODOR PAVLOVICH ZVONAREV

(1929 –   )

Fyodor Pavlovich Zvonarev was
born in the outskirts of Voronezh
in 1929. Zvonarev remembers always
wanting to be an artist. Like many
artists in that city, he started his art
career by working at the Voronezh
Theater, then moving on to studies
in Yeltsei and in St. Petersburg.
After graduation he moved to
Lipetsk, where he worked as an
artist for the musical theater. Soon,
however, spending most of his time
on designs for the theater tired him.
He yearned to leave the theater in
order to work exclusively as an easel
painter, which in 1961 he did.

Only landscape interests
Zvonarev as subject matter. He
investigates the changes in landscape at different seasons and times
of day, and experiments with
painting techniques. Traveling has
proved a great stimulant for this
painter. He has spent months at a
time around Lake Baikal and has
camped in Altai at Lake Sopky,
splitting rations with the local
bears. He enjoys painting the *taiga*.
Since joining the Artists' Union,
Zvonarev has been visiting the
Academic Dacha (about 150 km
from Moscow) as often as possible.
Artists gather at the dacha from all

Perreslavl-Zalesskiy
(outskirts of the
city), *1966. Oil on
panel. 17⅛ x 26 inches.*

over the former Soviet Union in groups of thirty at a time, which is how Zvonarev met artists from Vladimir whose distinctive style made an impression on him; their liberal use of paint and interpretative way with color encouraged him further in that direction.

Another influence on Zvonarev was the 1955 exhibition in Moscow of the work of the American painter Rockwell Kent. Says Zvonarev of that exhibit, "There were big canvases, huge canvases. I remember especially one of icebergs, and the color and surfaces were so beautiful. They were very close to my heart."

The Finley Collection's *Towers and Walls* (city of Pskov, Russia) by Zvonarev and Piotr Fomin's painting *Untitled,* of the same fortress in Pskov, provide an interesting comparison of two artists recording the same place in different styles.

Zvonarev's paintings are in collections in Denmark, France, Germany, Holland, Spain, the United States, and Russia. He exhibits often, both nationally and internationally.

Lady Summer, *1994.*
Oil on canvas.
23 ¹³/₁₆ x 31 ¾ inches.

ABOVE:
The End of
Summer, *1973.*
Oil on canvas.
21 ⅛ x 26 ⁷/₁₆ inches.

OPPOSITE:
Detail of The End of
Summer.

The Sunflowers Are
Blooming, *1992.*
Oil on canvas.
15 ⅛ x 22 inches.

OVERLEAF:
Detail of The
Sunflowers are
Blooming.

LEFT:
Towers and Walls
(city of Pskov,
Russia), *1995.*
Oil on canvas.
22 ½ x 29 ⅛ inches.

OPPOSITE:
Detail of Toward Spring.

RIGHT:
Spring Air, *1995.*
Oil on canvas.
23¹¹⁄₁₆ x 31½ inches.

BELOW:
Baikal Awakening,
1986. Oil on canvas.
17⁷⁄₁₆ x 23¼ inches.

OVERLEAF:
Detail of Spring Air.

NOTES FOR MARIA GOUGH ESSAY

1. "Piataia sessiia Akademii Khudozhestv SSSR," *Iskusstvo* 3 (1953): 3; quoted in Elena Kornetchuk, "Soviet Art and the State," in *The Quest for Self-Expression: Painting in Moscow and Leningrad, 1965–1990* (Columbus, Ohio: Columbus Museum of Art, 1990), 16–17.

2. See the excerpt from Andrei Zhadanov's speech to the First All-Union Congress of Soviet Writers in 1934, in *Russian Art of the Avant-Garde: Theory and Criticism, 1902–1934*, trans. and ed. John Bowlt, rev. and enl. ed. (New York: Thames and Hudson, 1988), 293. For a more complex and nuanced portrait of the phenomenon of Socialist Realism, which seeks to challenge the standard, reductive account of Stalinist cultural endeavor as singular and monolithic in focus, see Régine Robin, *Socialist Realism: An Impossible Aesthetic*, trans. Catherine Porter (Stanford: Stanford University Press, 1992).

3. It should be noted, in this connection, that the Russian terms *underground* and *aboveground* are not strictly interchangeable with *avant-garde* and *academic*, oppositional terms commonly used in the West. Rather, they explicitly acknowledge the role that the Soviet state has had in the control of artistic production and consumption. The role of the state in the constitution and operations of academies in general is discussed in Nikolaus Pevsner, *Academies of Art Past and Present* (1940; reprint, New York: Da Capo Press, 1973); and more recently, in two important essay collections: Anton Boschloo et al., eds., *Academies of Art between Renaissance and Romanticism* (The Hague: Stichting Leids Kunsthistorisch Jaarboek, 1989), and the special issue on "National Academies in Europe 1860–1906," *Art History* 20, no. 1 (March 1997).

4. See Karen-edis Barzman, "The Florentine Accademia del Disegno: Liberal Education and the Renaissance Artist," in Boschloo et al., *Academies of Art between Renaissance and Romanticism*, 14–32.

5. Vincenzo Danti, *Trattato delle perfette proporzioni* (1567), quoted and trans. in David Summers, *Michelangelo and the Language of Art* (Princeton: Princeton University Press, 1981), 279.

6. For this famous episode, see Dmitri Sarabianov, *Russian Art from Neoclassicism to the Avant-Garde* (New York: Harry N. Abrams, 1990), 104.

7. Pevsner, *Academies of Art*, vii–ix, 293.

8. This is the canonical account of modernist painting's quest for self-definition in terms of the properties of the medium itself; see Clement Greenberg, "Modernist Painting" (1960), in Greenberg, *The Collected Essays and Criticism* (Chicago: University of Chicago Press, 1986), vol. 4, 85–93. For a different account, see Leo Steinberg's incisive observations in his essay "Other Criteria," in *Other Criteria: Confrontations with Twentieth-Century Art* (London: Oxford University Press, 1976), 68–77.

9. See Albert Boime, "Curriculum Vitae: The Course of Life in the Nineteenth Century," in *Strictly Academic: Life Drawing in the Nineteenth Century* (Binghamton, N.Y.: University Art Gallery, S.U.N.Y., 1974), 5, 13; and idem, *The Academy and French Painting in the Nineteenth Century* (New Haven: Yale University Press, 1986).

10. For a study of modern copying practices, see Roger Benjamin, "Recovering Authors: The Modern Copy, Copy Exhibitions and Matisse," *Art History* 12, no. 2 (June 1989).

11. See Ellen Landau, *Jackson Pollock* (New York: Harry N. Abrams, 1989), 29–31.

12. For the debate concerning modernism and originality, see Rosalind Krauss, "The Originality of the Avant-Garde," in *The Originality of the Avant-Garde and Other Modernist Myths* (Cambridge, Mass.: MIT Press, 1985), 151–70.

13. The literature on this subject is vast, but see especially Fredric Jameson, *Postmodernism, or, The Cultural Logic of Late Capitalism* (Durham, N.C.: Duke University Press, 1991), chap. 1; and Douglas Crimp, *On the Museum's Ruins* (Cambridge, Mass.: MIT Press, 1993), 44–64, 126–37.

14. The terms are Crimp's; see *On the Museum's Ruins*, 126.

SOURCES FOR MELISSA HEFFERLIN ESSAY

The author drew on the following sources for the preparation of her essay:

Bown, Matthew. *Contemporary Russian Art*. New York: Phaidon, 1989.

Brummer, Hans Henrik. *Anders Zorn*. Stockholm: Norstedts, 1994.

Elkin, Vladimir. "Voronezh." [Cited April 2, 1997]. Available from http://www.vorstu.ac.ru/engl/city/koi/html.

Fomin, Nikita. Interview by author, September 1995, February 8 and 13, 1997.

Fomina, Marianna Borisovna. Interview by author, February 8, 1997.

Grishina, E. V., and A. A. Mazhaeva, eds. *Dva Veka Russkoi Khudozhestvennoi Shkoly* (Two centuries of Russian art school). Leningrad: Iskusstvo, 1991.

Kalyuta, Yura. Interview by author, February 8, 1997.

Kemenov, Vladimir. *The USSR Academy of Arts*. Leningrad: Aurora, 1982.

Korogodsky, Danila. Telephone conversation with author, April 4, 1997.

Kurbanov, Yaroslav. Interview by author, February 6, 1997.

Milner, John. *A Dictionary of Russian and Soviet Artists*. Suffolk: Antique Collectors' Club, 1993.

Mylnikov, Andrei. Interview by author, February 12, 1997.

Proshkin, Vladimir. Interview by author, February 7, 1997.

Repin, Sergei. Interview by author, February 13, 1997.

Repin, Nikolai. Interview by author, February 13, 1997.

Repkina, Veronica. Interview by author, February 11, 1997.

Safranova, Irina. Telephone conversation with author, December 16, 1996, and interview by author, February 8, 1997.

Sokolov, Leonid. Interview by author, February 6, 1997.

Sukhov, Vasily. Interview by author, February 13, 1997.

Terentyeva, Svetlana Arkadyevna. Interview by author, February 12 and 14, 1997.

Thieme, Ulrich, and Felix Becker. *Allgemeines Lexikon der Bildenden Kunstler*. Vol. 21. Leipzig: Seeman, 1956.

Trunov, Nikolai. Telephone conversation with author, January 6, 1997.

Vasilkovsky, Vladimir Mikhailovich. Interview by author, February 12, 1997.

APPENDIX 1: HISTORY OF THE REPIN INSTITUTE, ST. PETERSBURG

from 1718   Akademiya khudozhestv
(Academy of Art)

by 1884   Vysshaya khudozhestvennaya shkola (Higher Art School)

April–August 1918   Svobodnaya khudozhestvennaya shkola (Free Art School)

1918–21   Petrogradskie gosudarstvennye svobodnye khudozhestvenno-uchebnye masterskie (Petrograd State Free Art-School Studios)

1921–22   Petrogradskie vysshii gosudarstvennyi khudozhestvenno-tekhnicheskii masterskie (Petrograd Higher State Art-Technical Studios)

1922–24   Petrogradskii vysshii gosudarstvennyi khudozhestvenno-tekhnicheskii institut (Petrograd Higher State Art-Technical Institute)

1924–30   Leningradskii vysshii khudozhestvenno-tekhnicheskii institut (Leningrad Higher Art-Technical Institute)

1930–32   Institut proletarskogo izobrazitel'nogo iskusstva (Institute of Proletariat Fine Art)

June–December 1932   Leningradskii institut zhivopisi, skul'ptury i arkhitektury (Leningrad Institute of Painting, Sculpture, and Architecture)

1933–44   Institut zhivopisi, scul'ptury i arkhitektury (Institute of Painting, Sculpture, and Architecture)

1944–57   Institut zhivopisi, skul'ptury i arkhitektury imeni I. E. Repina (Repin Institute of Painting, Sculpture, and Architecture)

1957–91   Ordena Trudovogo Krasnogo Znameni Institut zhivopisi, skul'ptury i arkhitektury imeni I. E. Repina (Order of the Red Flag of Labor Repin Institute of Painting, Sculpture, and Architecture)

1997–   Sankt Peterburgskii gosudarstvennyi akademicheskii institut zhivopisi, skul'ptury i arkhitektury imeni I. E. Repina (The St. Petersburg State Academic Repin Institute of Painting, Sculpture, and Architecture)

From D. A. Safaralieva, *Uchebnyi Risunok v Akademii Khudozhestv* (Student drawing in the Academy of Art) (Moscow: Isobrazitel'noe iskusstvo, 1990), 158.

APPENDIX 2: HISTORY OF THE SURIKOV INSTITUTE, MOSCOW

from 1865   Moskovskaya Shkola (Moscow School)

by 1905   Moskovskaya shkola zhivopisi, skul'ptury i arkhitektury (Moscow School of Painting, Sculpture, and Architecture)

1923–25   Moskovskie vysshie khudozhestvenno-tekhnicheskie masterskie (Moscow Higher Art-Technical Studios)

1930s   Moskovskii vysshie khudozhestvenno-technicheskii institut (Moscow Higher Art-Technical Institute)

1947–48   Moskovskii gosudarstvennyi khudozhestvennyi institut (Moscow State Art Institute)

1948–57   Moskovskii gosudarstvennyi khudozhestvennyi institut imeni V. I. Surikova (Moscow State Surikov Art Institute)

1957–90   Moskovskii gosudarstvennyi Ordena Trudovogo Krasnogo Znameni khudozhestvennyi institut imeni V. I. Surikova (Moscow State Order of the Red Flag of Labor Surikov Art Institute)

From Vladimir Kemenov, *The USSR Academy of Arts* (Leningrad: Aurora, 1982), 33; and Safaralieva, *Uchebnyi Risunok* (Student drawing), 158.

ACKNOWLEDGEMENTS

We would like to thank the following individuals for their contributions to this book: Glen McGee, George Connor, Rosemary Dibben, Ruth Garren, and Crystal Bartusek.

All paintings were photographed by Raymond Martinot, except the one by Jim Madden on page 25 and those by Max McKenzie on pages 46, 77, 94 (top left), 97 (bottom right), 97 (top right), 130, 153, 158−59, 168, 169, 170, 172, 180, and 184 (top).

This book has been produced by CommonPlace Publishing. The text has been set in Centaur, a type designed in 1929 by Bruce Rogers, the most respected of American type designers. This classic letter is derived from the fifteenth century designs of the Venetian printer Nicolas Jensen. The display, however, is a more modern letter, Bremen, based upon European poster types produced during 1920−1940.

In 1995, Tennessee businessman and art collector Lyle Finley discovered a wealth of painting that had long been locked behind the Iron Curtain. He immediately responded to this art made by Russian academy-trained artists, dedicated to the creation of beautiful, sincere works employing superlative technique.

Assembled since the collapse of the Soviet Union, the Finley Collection juxtaposes works by some of Russia's most distinguished older artists with that of its newest, brightest talents. Dating from the 1940s to the late 1990s, the artwork in the Finley Collection displays a range of subjects — landscapes, portraits, still lifes, rural scenes, cityscapes — made in a variety of media, including oil on canvas; watercolor, gouache, sepia, charcoal, and pencil on paper; bronze; and glazed porcelain. They are presented in 181 colorplates, including many full-page and double-spread details.

The artists themselves come from many of the different nations that made up the Soviet Union. All, however, share a Russian academic art training and its commitment to technical accomplishment and the interpretation of nature. This tradition dates back almost two and a half centuries in Russia and shows every sign of continuing to be a dynamic force far into the future. These are elements that set these artists apart from their Western contemporaries.

Melissa Hefferlin, the only American to study at perhaps the most prestigious of Russia's academies, the Repin Institute, St. Petersburg, during the Soviet period, has written an absorbing and highly informative account of the Russian institutes. We learn in detail the rigorous training these artists undergo as well as their past and current